RESILIENT

Resilient: Leading Beyond Metrics

ISBN: 9798345589465

Copyright © 2024 by Garrick Thomas

All rights reserved.

First printing, December, 2024

No portion of this book may be reproduced in any form without written permission from the publisher or author, except as permitted by U.S. copyright law.

DISCLAIMER

This book provides information regarding organizational resilience and leadership. It is sold with the understanding that the author and publisher are not rendering professional services.

While the author and publisher have used their best efforts in preparing this work, they make no representations or warranties regarding its contents and assume no liability for its use. Readers should consult appropriate professionals for advice specific to their situations.

Neither the publisher nor the author shall be liable for any loss of profit or any other commercial damages, including but not limited to special, incidental, consequential, personal, or other damages.

Resilient

Leading Beyond Metrics

How Great Leaders Build Adaptive Organizations

Garrick Thomas

CONTENTS

Preface ix

Chapter 1   Why Traditional Resilience Fails 1

Chapter 2   Understanding Ends, Ways, and Means 9

Chapter 3   The Fundamentals of Resilient Organizations 19

Chapter 4   Starting Your Resilience Journey 41

Chapter 5   Resilience in the Age of Generative AI 51

Chapter 6   Selecting and Promoting Resilient Leaders 69

Chapter 7   Systems Thinking and Resilience 93

Chapter 8   The Reality of Resilience 109

Chapter 9   Resilience for Smaller Organizations 127

Chapter 10   Conclusion 137

References 141
Index 149

PREFACE

When a measure becomes a target, it ceases to be a good measure.
- Goodhart's Law

Let's go back to 2014, when Satya Nadella took over Microsoft. He inherited a company trapped by its own metrics. Revenue was strong, and Windows dominated the PC market. By every metric that Microsoft's board and C-suite measured, what was wrong? Well, other than solid metrics, Microsoft had missed mobile computing, fallen behind in cloud technology, and were rapidly losing relevance in a changing world. What happened next reveals the crucial difference between metric-focused leadership and true resilience. Instead of pushing harder on existing metrics, Nadella fundamentally transformed how Microsoft operated, measured success, and built capability. The result? Microsoft's value soared from $300 billion to over $3 trillion, establishing them as a leader in cloud computing and AI. This wasn't just about better numbers—it was about building an organization that could adapt, evolve, and thrive through constant disruption.

For over twenty years, I've had the privilege of being in the room where critical organizational decisions are shaped—executive meetings where directors set strategy, briefing rooms where military commanders shape operational targets, and government offices where ministers outline their governance objectives. This unique vantage point has given me a clear view of how decisions at both governance and execution levels impact an organization's future, and what truly determines success or failure in times of disruption.

As a perpetual student of leadership, I closely observed their words, decisions, reasoning, and logic. Not to judge, but to understand the rationale behind their choices. What emerged was a clear pattern: when leaders at both board and C-suite levels faced a choice between building long-term resilience or hitting the next short-term metric—they almost always chose the metric. In fact, in over two decades of witnessing high-stakes decisions in boardrooms and command centers, I can recall only a handful of times when a senior leader deliberately chose long-term strategy over immediate metrics. The overwhelming response was always some version of "yes, I am aware that there is a risk on the horizon, but right now the organization needs to focus on hitting this near-term objective." Now that may be a valid response, but when it is always the response, we end up with those same leaders later appearing dismayed when the very disruptions they had downplayed materialized. It is an art unto itself, to sit quietly in meetings where senior leaders struggled to explain why an abrupt pivot was now required to address the exact disruptions they had earlier dismissed. Boards, tasked with long-term strategic oversight, often defaulted to quarterly performance reviews. C-suites, taking their cue from their boards, doubled down on short-term operational metrics. It creates a vicious cycle that amplifies short-term thinking at every level.

So I had to start asking, is there a better way? Is there a way to look beyond metrics, and do what is best for the long-term benefit of an organization. I mean what good is the quarterly bonus if you're out of a job or business the next year? I offer this with the understanding that metrics are in fact needed; they are not going anywhere. You need to have metrics to know if you are on your intended path. But the issue is that so many organizations make achieving the metric unto itself the path, and build around it. And metrics by and large tend to be short-term focused: new customers, revenue growth, customer support ticket times, account retention ratio, and on and on. But what so many leaders miss is that metrics alone, are neither proper end state targets for organizational resilience, nor even if achieved, indicators of stability. We can see how much metric successes did not represent proper resilience if we look at 2020, because…

Then came COVID, the mother of all disruptors, and it provided a stark demonstration of the gap between disruption and resilience planning. At the board level, where pandemic-scale disruption should have been part of strategic oversight, there was no real planning. At the C-suite level, where such plans should have been operationalized, there was only tactical response. If your board's idea of resilience is letting the

C-suite figure it out, and your C-suite's idea is that everyone will just work harder, you need to understand that working harder is not resilience -- it's compensation for lack of strategic foresight and operational planning.

But it has been more than COVID. The past two decades have challenged governance and operational fundamentals at every level. Boards faced new strategic imperatives they weren't prepared for, while C-suites struggled to transform their organizations fast enough. We've experienced dot-com crashes, housing market meltdowns, supply chain disruptions, a global pandemic, AI transformation, and fundamental changes in how work gets done. Each of these events tested not just operational resilience, but the very framework of how boards guide their organizations and how C-suites execute that guidance.

And from all of this, it became clear that the adaptive mindset is what I had seen lacking at both governance and executive levels. Boards, or their equivalents, frequently failed to set strategic direction for long-term resilience, defaulting instead to quarterly oversight. C-suites, in turn, focused on immediate adaptation rather than building lasting capability. Yeah, they can adapt to what is in front of them, but I'm talking about board-directed, C-suite-implemented, beyond-the-horizon adaptation that lets organizations thrive when disruption attempts to strike -- not just muddle through.

What Will You Get From This Book

This book presents a different way leaders can drive organizations. It's intended for those who want to move beyond metric-focused approaches toward improved resilience that delivers results even in disruption. I've kept the narrative straight-forward, avoiding unnecessary technical or academic diversions. Drawing from real-world examples of organizational success and failure, it serves as an entry point for board directors setting resilience strategy, C-suite executives implementing that strategy, and leaders at other levels making resilient decisions. It recognizes that traditional approaches to organizational stability no longer suffice in today's rapidly changing environment, and that success requires clear delineation between the board's role in directing resilience strategy and the C-suite's role in executing it. Through examining specific cases - from

Microsoft's AI transformation to Boeing's 737 MAX crisis - we'll explore practical lessons for both boards and C-suites in their distinct but complementary roles.

My goal isn't to provide an exhaustive transformation manual, nor am I dismissive of metrics—organizations must measure progress. I recognize that achieving positive results is essential for survival and prosperity. But consider this: what good is a victory today if it sets you up for failure tomorrow? That's why I aim to demonstrate that achieving metrics alone, or treating them as an end state, falls far short of true resilience. When an organization assigns a metric, it drives operational and financial decisions down-chain toward an end state that's often bound to a narrow, short-term understanding of success. As you read these chapters, be prepared to think deeply about your organization. This isn't like assembling IKEA furniture, where fixed components and specific steps guarantee a final product; neither I nor anyone outside your world can prescribe the exact steps your organization needs. While this book will show you how to build resilience and adaptive capabilities, you must work out the implementation details.

This book offers essential insights into what real resilience looks like, structured specifically for both board directors setting direction and C-suite executives implementing strategies. I've favored concise examples, points, and lists over long narratives. Each chapter is crafted for quick understanding and easy reference. Clear delineation between board-level decisions and C-suite implementation allows readers to focus on their specific roles while grasping the complete resilience picture. Above all, this serves as a starting point for leaders ready to move beyond traditional metrics and build organizations capable of adapting to whatever challenges arise.

While I use the terms board-level and C-suite throughout the text, they convey organizational levels in common terms. See board-level as those setting strategy, and C-suite as those executing it – groups every organization has, regardless of labels. Whether you're in a startup with a small leadership team, a military unit with command structures, or a government agency with oversight boards, this division between those who set strategic direction and those who execute it exists. The principles of resilience apply regardless of how these levels are formally titled.

The choice to build resilience isn't easy. It requires challenging short-term performance, transforming operations and culture, and rethinking how we measure success. At every leadership level, this demands not just understanding what needs to be done, but having the courage to do it. Leaders face difficult trade-offs at every turn. But as the examples will show, it's a choice that increasingly separates organizations that thrive from those that fail.

Garrick Thomas
2024

1

WHY TRADITIONAL RESILIENCE FAILS

Let me tell you about Lehman Brothers' last 24 hours.

September 14, 2008: Their board was reviewing what looked like solid governance. Their C-suite was presenting what appeared to be strong operational numbers. A 158-year-old Wall Street institution. The fourth-largest investment bank in America. Their board-approved risk management systems? State of the art. C-suite crisis readiness? By the book. Balance sheet? According to all traditional metrics at both governance and operational levels, manageable.

By sunrise the next day, Lehman Brothers was bankrupt. $600 billion in assets, gone. 25,000 employees suddenly without jobs. The largest bankruptcy in American history.

This wasn't just a failure - it was a catastrophic demonstration of how traditional approaches to resilience can create a dangerous illusion of security. The board had every traditional governance oversight system in place. The C-suite had every traditional risk management protocol running. What they didn't have? Actual resilience.

If you're sitting there thinking, "But we have sophisticated risk models" or "Our stress tests are comprehensive," I need you to pay close attention to what comes next. Because here's the truth that most leaders don't want to hear: The old ways of building resilience are dead. They just don't know it yet.

What happened at Lehman Brothers reveals a critical distinction in resilience failure. At the board level, directors focused on governance metrics that showed strong oversight but missed strategic vulnerabilities. At the C-suite level, executives executed flawlessly against the wrong priorities. This pattern - boards failing to direct true resilience strategy and C-suites failing to build adaptive capabilities - repeats across nearly every major organizational collapse.

The False Promise of Traditional Resilience

Let's get real about what passes for "resilience" in most organizations today. You've got your crisis response plans sitting in a binder somewhere. You've got your quarterly risk assessments that everyone dutifully fills out. You've got your metrics and KPIs that make everything look neat and tidy. And it's all about as useful as a paperweight in a hurricane.

Take Nokia. In 2007, they dominated the global mobile phone market with a 49.4% share. Their board saw strong market position, approved healthy financials, and reviewed detailed contingency plans. Their C-suite maintained robust supply chains and executed traditional resilience metrics flawlessly. Then Apple launched the iPhone. By 2013, Nokia's market share had plummeted to 3%, leading to a fire sale of their mobile division to Microsoft for a fraction of its former value. The board had failed to set strategic direction for mobile evolution, while the C-suite failed to build the capabilities needed to adapt to market transformation.

The problem wasn't that Nokia couldn't see the iPhone coming - they saw it. The problem was that their traditional approach to resilience focused on protecting their existing business model rather than adapting to a fundamentally changing market. They were measuring all the wrong things, tracking irrelevant metrics, and following outdated playbooks.

Or look at Blockbuster in 2010. They had crisis plans. They had risk matrices. They had decades of market dominance. What they didn't have was the ability to adapt when Netflix changed the game. Their traditional resilience metrics showed a healthy business right up until they filed for bankruptcy. Why? Because they were measuring stability when they should have been measuring adaptability.

Here's what traditional resilience gets fundamentally wrong:
1. It prioritizes protecting the status quo over adapting to change
2. It mistakes compliance for capability
3. It focuses on avoiding failure rather than building adaptive capacity
4. It values measuring things over understanding them

The most dangerous part? This false sense of security actively prevents organizations from developing real resilience. It's like having sophisticated

WHY TRADITIONAL RESILIENCE FAILS

radar systems to detect icebergs while ignoring the fact that your ship can't turn quickly enough to avoid them.

The Sustainability Deception

Leaders often mistake their organization's ability to power through disruption as evidence of resilience. This "Sustainability Deception" manifests in multiple ways: demanding longer hours from workers, slashing prices to maintain market share, squeezing suppliers for short-term savings, or cutting corners on quality to hit targets. While these brute-force approaches might generate immediate results, they fundamentally weaken the organization's ability to sustain performance or withstand future disruptions.

Consider how Circuit City responded to competition from Best Buy in the early 2000s. Their leadership fired their highest-paid (and most experienced) sales staff to cut costs, pushed remaining workers harder, and competed primarily on price. Initially, their metrics improved—costs dropped, margins stabilized, stock price rose. But this illusion of resilience through brute force proved catastrophic. Customer service deteriorated, employee morale collapsed, and their ability to adapt to market changes vanished. By 2009, a once-dominant retailer with $12 billion in annual revenues ceased to exist.

Even as customer experience deteriorated and market position weakened, Circuit City doubled down on cost-cutting and traditional efficiency metrics—a perfect example of the sunk cost fallacy in organizational decision-making. Rather than adapt their approach based on mounting evidence of failure, they invested more heavily in measuring and managing the very metrics that were destroying their capability to compete. It's the organizational equivalent of throwing good resources after bad, hoping that somehow measuring the same things more intensively will produce different results.

Similar patterns emerge across industries. Airlines that respond to disruption by cramming more seats into planes, cutting staff training, and degrading service standards might see short-term profit improvements. Yet this approach inevitably leads to operational breakdowns, customer dissatisfaction, and vulnerability to competitors who invest in building real systemic capability. United Airlines learned this lesson painfully in 2017 when their cost-cutting and aggressive overbooking practices led to the infamous passenger removal incident, destroying billions in market value overnight.

Even tech companies fall prey to this deception. Game developer CD Projekt Red, facing delays with their highly anticipated Cyberpunk 2077 game, pushed their developers through months of "crunch time"—mandatory overtime and weekend work. The result? A bug-filled release that damaged their reputation, triggered refunds, and saw their stock price plummet 75%. They achieved their release date target but sacrificed the very capabilities—quality, innovation, and talent retention—needed for long-term success.

The alternative to this deception is building true systemic resilience. When Satya Nadella took over Microsoft, he didn't demand more effort from an already hardworking workforce. Instead, he transformed how the organization functioned as a system—changing culture, rebuilding processes, and developing new capabilities. This systems thinking approach didn't just deliver better results; it created sustainable performance that strengthens rather than depletes the organization. The lesson is clear: leaders who mistake intensity for resilience aren't just failing to solve their problems—they're actively undermining their organization's ability to survive future challenges.

Today's Reality: The New Normal

The business landscape of 2024 bears little resemblance to the world where traditional resilience models were developed. Consider this: Boeing, a company that epitomized traditional approaches to quality and safety, found itself in crisis with the 737 MAX. Despite having some of the most rigorous safety protocols in the industry, their traditional resilience frameworks failed to prevent or adequately address a crisis that cost lives and billions in market value.

Why? Because today's challenges don't play by yesterday's rules. We're operating in what military strategists call a VUCA environment - Volatile, Uncertain, Complex, and Ambiguous. And if you think that's just consultant-speak, let me break it down with real numbers:

WHY TRADITIONAL RESILIENCE FAILS

- The average lifespan of a company on the S&P 500 has dropped from 61 years in 1958 to less than 18 years today.
- 52% of Fortune 500 companies from 2000 are now gone - either bankrupt, acquired, or fallen off the list.
- The time it takes for a new technology to reach 50 million users has shrunk from 75 years for the telephone to just 19 days for Pokémon Go.

The speed of change isn't just numbers on a chart - it's reshaping how disruption happens. Look at how Airbnb disrupted the hotel industry. Major hotel chains had traditional resilience plans for everything from economic downturns to natural disasters. What they weren't prepared for? A platform that could add more rooms than the largest hotel chains without owning a single property.

That's today's reality. The threats don't come in neat packages that fit your risk matrix. They come from angles your traditional metrics can't even measure.

The Hidden Costs of False Resilience

Let me show you what this looks like in real money. BlackBerry (formerly RIM) had $20 billion in revenue in 2011, dominant market share, and every traditional measure of business resilience in place. Their executives were so confident in their position that they dismissed the iPhone as a toy. We know how that ended - by 2016, their hardware revenue had dropped to zero.

But here's what you might not know: The real costs started long before the revenue dropped. They showed up as:

1. Organizational Blind Spots

Remember Kodak? They actually invented the digital camera in 1975. But their traditional metrics focused on protecting their film business. The cost? A 130-year-old company in bankruptcy by 2012.

2. Resource Misallocation

General Electric spent $4 billion building a "digital transformation" initiative based on traditional corporate resilience thinking. The result? A

75% decline in market value between 2016 and 2019 because they were solving yesterday's problems with yesterday's mindset.

3. Lost Opportunities

Borders Books had the chance to buy Amazon's e-commerce platform in 2001. Their traditional risk metrics said sticking to physical stores was safer. By 2011, they were liquidating everything - including the bookshelves.

4. Cultural Calcification

Xerox PARC invented most of the technologies that made personal computing possible - the graphical user interface, the mouse, ethernet. But their traditional corporate structure and metrics couldn't capitalize on any of it. Instead, Steve Jobs walked in, saw the future, and the rest is Apple's history.

Signs Your Organization Needs a New Approach

Right now, you might be thinking, 'But we're different. Our governance is solid. Our operations are comprehensive.' That's exactly what Sears thought too. Let's do a quick reality check. The signs of inadequate resilience manifest differently at governance and execution levels, but both signal an organization stuck in traditional thinking.

At the Board Level:
- Strategic oversight focuses primarily on quarterly performance
- Risk assessment emphasizes compliance over adaptation
- Innovation oversight lacks clear direction
- Strategy discussions center on protecting current position
- Succession planning prioritizes maintaining status quo

At the C-Suite Level:
- Success metrics haven't changed in the last five years
- Risk assessments focus more on protection than adaptation
- Innovation happens despite processes, not because of them
- Response to disruption starts with 'According to our manual...'

WHY TRADITIONAL RESILIENCE FAILS

- Implementation prioritizes efficiency over resilience

The presence of even a few of these signs at either level indicates systemic vulnerability to disruption. When they appear at both levels, the organization isn't just exposed - it's actively reinforcing its own fragility

A New Path Forward

You might be wondering, "If traditional resilience is dead, what replaces it?" That's the right question, but before I give you the answer, let me tell you about Microsoft under Satya Nadella.

When Nadella took over in 2014, Microsoft was still playing defense. They had every traditional resilience measure in place - strong balance sheet, risk management systems, crisis plans, the works. But they were losing ground in mobile, missing the cloud revolution, and watching their Windows empire slowly erode.

What Nadella did next wasn't in any traditional resilience playbook. He didn't double down on protecting Windows. He didn't launch another risk management initiative. Instead, he did something that probably looked crazy to traditional metrics: He embraced competitive platforms, pushed Microsoft into the cloud, and fundamentally changed how the company thought about resilience.

The result? Microsoft's market value increased from $300 billion to over $3 trillion. More importantly, they built something traditional resilience could never deliver: the ability to thrive on change rather than just survive it.

That's what adaptive resilience looks like. It's not about building higher walls - it's about building better wings.

In the chapters ahead, we're going to explore exactly how to build those wings. You'll learn:

- Why the Ends, Ways, and Means framework is replacing traditional strategic planning
  - The five fundamental shifts that make organizations truly resilient
  - How to start your own resilience transformation
  - How to lead resilience as organizations adapt AI

- The best ways to select resilient-minded talent for leadership roles
- How to apply resilience to smaller organizations

But first, you need to make a choice. You can keep clinging to traditional resilience metrics, writing more detailed crisis plans, and measuring more sophisticated risk indicators. That's what Blockbuster did right up until Netflix ate their lunch.

Or you can accept that the game has changed. That traditional resilience is like bringing a knife to a gunfight - it might make you feel armed, but it won't keep you alive.

The old playbook is dead. In the chapters ahead, we'll write a new one together.

2

UNDERSTANDING ENDS, WAYS, AND MEANS

Let's start with Ford Motor Company in 2006. The company was hemorrhaging money - $12.7 billion in losses that year alone. Traditional metrics screamed for cost-cutting, layoffs, and divestment. Instead, new CEO Alan Mulally did something that probably looked insane at the time: He borrowed $23.6 billion against everything Ford owned, including the blue oval logo itself.

But here's what most people miss about that story. Mulally wasn't just raising cash - he was implementing what military strategists call the Ends, Ways, and Means framework. Let me break down how this actually works, because it's probably not what you think.

Think of it like this: When the U.S. military plans an operation, they don't start with "what resources do we have?" or even "what's our strategy?" They start with the end state - what has to be true when we're done? Then they figure out how to get there (Ways), and finally what they need to make it happen (Means).

Mulally did the exact same thing at Ford:

Ends: Build vehicles people want while returning to profitability

Ways: Simplify the product line, modernize manufacturing, unify global operations

Means: That $23.6 billion loan and every asset Ford could leverage

The result? When the 2008 financial crisis hit and every other U.S. automaker needed a government bailout, Ford survived on its own. By 2010, they posted a $6.6 billion profit.

The Ends, Ways, and Means framework maps perfectly to organizational hierarchy. Boards must own and direct the Ends - they're responsible for setting strategic direction and defining what resilience means for the organization. The C-suite owns the Ways and Means -

they're accountable for determining how to achieve those Ends and what resources to deploy. This clear delineation of responsibilities is crucial for building true resilience.

Let's Get Real About Ends

Here's where both boards and C-suites fundamentally misunderstand their roles in setting goals - they confuse metrics with Ends. When Microsoft was struggling in 2014, their board saw metrics that looked fine: Windows dominated PCs, Office was everywhere, cash reserves were strong. The C-suite executed flawlessly against these metrics. But these weren't Ends - they were just numbers. The board needed to set strategic direction beyond metrics, which they finally achieved under Nadella's leadership. The C-suite, in turn, needed to build capabilities beyond metric achievement, which Nadella's team executed brilliantly.

Think about Apple for a minute. Their board didn't set an End of 'sell more iPhones' - they set a strategic direction to 'create technology that empowers people and enriches their lives.' Amazon's board didn't set an End to 'grow e-commerce revenue' - they established 'to be Earth's most customer-centric company.' See the difference? These are board-level strategic directives that give C-suites clear direction while allowing them flexibility in how to achieve these Ends. The separation of duties is clear: boards set aspirational, strategic Ends; C-suites determine the Ways and Means to achieve them.

Real Ends transcend metrics. They answer the question: "What has to be true for us to matter in the future?"

Let me show you what this looks like in practice. When Anne Mulcahy took over Xerox in 2001, the company was near bankruptcy. Traditional metrics said cut costs, sell assets, protect the core business. Instead, she defined an End that went beyond numbers: transform Xerox from a copier company into a technology and services leader that helped businesses work better.

That End drove everything else. It's why she cut 80% of products but increased R&D spending. It's why she invested in services when everyone said stick to hardware. By 2009, Xerox was thriving not because they hit metric targets, but because they achieved their End.

UNDERSTANDING ENDS, WAYS, AND MEANS

Here's what real Ends look like:
- They transcend quarterly performance
- They drive adaptation rather than just protection
- They answer "why we exist" not just "what we do"
- They inspire action rather than just measure activity

Understanding Ways

Ways are how you achieve your Ends, but here's where most organizations go wrong - they mistake activities for Ways. Let me show you what I mean.

When Reed Hastings transformed Netflix from a DVD-by-mail service into a streaming giant, he didn't just list activities like "build streaming platform" or "create original content." He developed Ways that fundamentally changed how the company operated:
- Shift from content distribution to content creation
- Build a data-driven understanding of viewer preferences
- Create a culture of constant innovation

These weren't just tasks to check off - they were systematic approaches to achieving Netflix's End of transforming entertainment.

Compare that to Blockbuster. Their "Ways" were just activities: improve store operations, optimize inventory, enhance customer service. They were doing things without actually changing how they operated. We know how that story ended.

Your Means Are Not What You Think

Here's where most organizations completely miss the point about Means. They think Means are just about resources - money, people, technology. But let me show you why that's dangerously wrong.

Take Toys "R" Us. In 2005, they had plenty of resources - 1,500 stores, billions in revenue, massive brand recognition. They even had an early partnership with Amazon for online sales. But they lacked the real Means that mattered: the ability to transform those resources into new capabilities.

Compare that to how Satya Nadella repositioned Microsoft's Means. Yes, Microsoft had massive resources, but Nadella understood that true Means are about capabilities, not just assets. He took Microsoft's existing resources and transformed them into new capabilities:
- Shifted from selling software to providing cloud services
- Transformed from a closed ecosystem to an open platform
- Converted traditional engineering talent into cloud-native developers

This is where the military's understanding of Means becomes crucial. When military planners talk about Means, they're not just counting tanks and troops - they're assessing capabilities and how they can be adapted to achieve the mission.

Making It All Work Together

Now here's the key that brings it all together - Ends, Ways, and Means must form what military strategists call a "strategic combination." Let me show you what this looks like in practice using Amazon.

Amazon's End: To be Earth's most customer-centric company

Ways:
- Relentless focus on customer experience
- Continuous innovation in service delivery
- Long-term thinking over short-term profits

Means:
- Technology infrastructure that can scale infinitely
- Culture of innovation and experimentation
- Operational systems that can adapt rapidly

See how each element reinforces the others while respecting organizational hierarchy? The board-directed End drives the C-suite's selection of Ways, which determines their deployment of Means, which enable their Ways to achieve the board's End. It's a continuous loop between governance and execution, not a linear process. The board sets direction and monitors progress, while the C-suite determines implementation and builds capabilities. When this governance-execution loop works properly, true resilience emerges.

But here's the warning: This isn't a one-and-done exercise. Look at how Apple's board and C-suite have evolved their strategic combination:

1976:
Board-Set End: Make computers accessible to everyone
C-Suite Ways: Simple design, user-friendly interfaces
C-Suite Means: Engineering talent, innovative design capabilities

2001:
Board-Set End: Revolution in personal technology
C-Suite Ways: Integrate hardware, software, and services
C-Suite Means: Design excellence, retail experience, ecosystem control

2024:
Board-Set End: Technology that enriches lives
C-Suite Ways: Seamless integration across devices and services
C-Suite Means: AI capabilities, privacy architecture, services infrastructure

The key is that while the board's fundamental End has evolved, the C-suite has dramatically transformed their Ways and Means to keep achieving it. This harmony between governance and execution creates sustainable resilience.

Real Leaders, Real Transformations

Let me show you what the Ends, Ways, and Means framework looks like in action through two leaders who got it right and one who spectacularly missed the point.

First, the failures - because sometimes you learn more from what goes wrong. Remember Ron Johnson at J.C. Penney? In 2011, he had a clear End: transform Penney's into an upscale shopping destination. Sounds good, right? But his Ways (eliminating discounts, reorganizing stores) and his Means (existing staff, traditional retail infrastructure) were completely misaligned. The result? A billion-dollar loss in his first year and his exit 17 months later.

Now let's look at success. When Satya Nadella took over Microsoft, he didn't just set an End of cloud dominance. He aligned everything:

End: Empower every person and organization to achieve more

Ways:
- Shift from "Windows first" to "cloud first"
- Transform culture from "know-it-all" to "learn-it-all"
- Build partnerships with former competitors

Means:
- Retrained engineering talent for cloud
- Rebuilt infrastructure for cloud services
- Restructured incentives to reward collaboration

The result? Microsoft's market value soared, but more importantly, they built true resilience through alignment.

Making It Work in Your Organization

Here's your practical roadmap for implementing this framework:

Step 1: Define Your Real End
Don't tell me about revenue targets or market share. Ask:
- What difference will we make in five years?
- Why will we matter to our customers?
- What capabilities will make us resilient?

Step 2: Identify Your Ways
- List everything you're doing now
- Ruthlessly eliminate anything that doesn't serve your End
- Add new Ways that will actually get you there

UNDERSTANDING ENDS, WAYS, AND MEANS

Step 3: Audit Your Means
- Be honest about your real capabilities (not just resources)
- Identify gaps between what you have and what you need
- Plan how to transform current Means into needed capabilities

The Hard Truth About Implementation

Let me be brutally honest - this isn't going to be easy. You'll face resistance. People love their metrics, their familiar processes, their comfortable ways of measuring success.

But here's what's at stake: Look at Kodak again. Their board set an End tied to dying technology (dominate photography), leaving their C-suite to pursue Ways (superior film technology) and deploy Means (manufacturing excellence) that couldn't adapt. The problem started at governance - the board failed to set an End that would force digital adaptation. This left the C-suite optimizing for the wrong future. When both governance and execution are misaligned with reality, failure is inevitable.

Don't be Kodak.

Monitoring Without Getting Lost in Metrics

Here's where most organizations go sideways - they turn right back to traditional metrics to monitor their Ends, Ways, and Means transformation. Let me show you a better approach through the lens of how Microsoft actually tracks their cloud transformation.

They don't just measure cloud revenue or customer acquisition. They track:
- How quickly teams can adapt to new customer needs?
- Where their capabilities are expanding or constraining growth?
- How effectively different parts of the organization can collaborate?

But let's get specific about what you should monitor:

Ends Alignment Check:
- Are your decisions actually serving your End or just hitting metrics?

- Do your people understand the End beyond the numbers?
- Is your End still relevant as markets change?

Ways Effectiveness:
- Which Ways are actually moving you toward your End?
- Where are you seeing resistance or bottlenecks?
- What new Ways are emerging from your teams?

Means Development:
- Are your capabilities growing or just your resources?
- Where are you seeing capability gaps?
- How quickly can you deploy resources in new ways?

The Power of Strategic Combinations

Remember when Apple decided to develop its own chips? That wasn't just a technology decision. Look at how it created a powerful strategic combination:

End: Control the entire user experience
Ways: Design custom silicon for specific Apple needs
Means: Chip design capability, manufacturing partnerships, integration expertise

The result? Not just better performance, but true resilience through deep capability development.

Making Course Corrections

Here's what separates great leaders from good ones - they know when to adjust the formula. Let me show you how this works in real time:
When COVID-19 hit, Microsoft didn't change their End. But they dramatically shifted their Ways and Means to:
- Accelerate Teams development
- Rebuild support systems for remote work
- Transform their own workforce while helping customers do the same

The Future of Resilience

Let me leave you with this: The world isn't getting any simpler or more predictable. The leaders who will thrive are those who can:
- Set Ends that matter beyond metrics
- Develop Ways that can evolve with circumstances
- Build Means that create true capabilities, not just resources

The evidence from organizations across industries we have looked at makes it clear how Ends, Ways, and Means, if used from the point of resilience design, works superior to a linear approach. Those organizations that kept on a linear, metric-driven path do not have the records of those that did not. Leaders in organizations can continue measuring what's comfortable and managing what's familiar or build the capabilities that create true resilience. For anyone in a leadership role at this point in the conditions of modern business disruption that choses to maintain a focus on metrics, treating them as ends rather than indicators – good luck.

3

THE FUNDAMENTALS OF RESILIENT ORGANIZATIONS

When we look at resilience and how it is achieved through leadership, while there are many aspects that we could discuss, there are certain fundamentals that stand out. They're not rocket science, just aspects that are consistently represented in leaders who get their organizations through disruption and challenges, and absent or incomplete in the approaches leaders take in organizations that failed. Let's jump back to 2020 to see a quick example.

March 2020: Both Zoom and Cisco's WebEx found themselves at the center of the biggest remote work experiment in history. Both had video conferencing technology. Both had enterprise customers. Both had years of experience. Both had capable boards and experienced C-suites.

But while WebEx struggled with scaling and customer complaints, Zoom went from 10 million to 300 million daily meeting participants. The difference? Zoom's board and C-suite understood what we're about to explore - the five fundamentals that separate truly resilient organizations from those just trying to survive. Their board set strategic direction for resilience, and their C-suite built the capabilities to deliver it. What follows is a framework for both governance and execution teams to build true organizational resilience.

Fundamental #1: Adaptive Leadership DNA

Leadership hierarchy, governance structures, and operational control are often mistaken for adaptive capability. Organizations see a strong board providing oversight, or a C-suite demonstrating command of operations, and believe this indicates resilience. This fundamental misunderstanding—confusing traditional leadership approaches with true adaptive capability—undermines organizations at both governance and execution levels. Moreover, the organizational structure itself—whether traditional hierarchy, flat organization, hybrid model, or small team-based—matters far less than how leadership leverages these structures to build resilience. A poorly placed leader, or leadership team misaligned with resilience thinking, will negate any adaptive advantages these structures might otherwise provide. To understand what real adaptive leadership looks like, and how it enables resilience, let's examine both levels.

When Ed Bastian took over as CEO of Delta Air Lines in 2016, the company was profitable but vulnerable. Delta's board empowered a fundamental shift in strategic direction - moving from pure performance oversight to resilience preparation. Bastian, with clear board mandate, did something most C-suites wouldn't - he started building adaptive capabilities before disruption hit. He:

- Invested in customer experience when competitors cut costs
- Built financial reserves when Wall Street wanted stock buybacks
- Strengthened employee relationships when labor was already stable

The result? When COVID-19 devastated the airline industry, Delta was the only major U.S. carrier that avoided the threat of bankruptcy.

But here's what most people miss about Bastian's approach. He wasn't just making good decisions - he was embedding adaptive capabilities into Delta's DNA. How?

- Decentralized decision-making to front-line managers
- Created rapid feedback loops between customers and operations
- Built multiple backup plans for every critical system

This isn't about having a great leader - it's about building leadership resilience into the organization itself.

Fundamental #2: Network-Centric Operations

Most organizations still operate like armies from the 1800s - boards focusing on rigid oversight structures while C-suites maintain strict hierarchies. Both levels hoard information and slow decision-making. Let me show you what network-centric operations actually looks like through

THE FUNDAMENTALS OF RESILIENT ORGANIZATIONS

Procter & Gamble's transformation, where their board redefined governance networks while their C-suite rebuilt operational ones.

In 2000, P&G was struggling despite having some of the world's strongest brands. Their traditional structure was killing innovation. CEO A.G. Lafley didn't just reorganize - he rewired how the entire company operated. He launched "Connect + Develop," opening P&G's innovation process to a global network of partners, suppliers, and even competitors.

The result? Over 50% of P&G's product innovations now come from external collaborations. But here's the key insight most people miss: This wasn't just about open innovation - it was about building a networked organization that could:
- Sense market changes faster than competitors
- Mobilize resources across organizational boundaries
- Adapt faster than traditional hierarchies

Think about how Toyota handled the 2011 tsunami that devastated its supply chain. Their network-centric approach meant they:
- Had visibility into multiple tiers of suppliers
- Could quickly identify alternative sources
- Could share solutions across their entire network

They recovered months faster than competitors who relied on traditional, hierarchical supply chain management.

Fundamental #3: Rapid Experimentation Culture

Here's where most organizations get experimentation completely wrong - boards treat it like risk management while C-suites treat it like a lab experiment. True resilience requires evolutionary adaptation at both levels. Look at how Amazon approaches experimentation:

Board Level:
- Sets strategic tolerance for experimentation
- Measures success through capability building, not just ROI
- Evaluates quarterly results through learning lens

C-Suite Level:

- Runs continuous operational experiments
- Treats failure as data, not disaster
- Measures learning cycles in days, not quarters

Jeff Bezos put it perfectly: "If you know in advance that it's going to work, it's not an experiment."

But here's the critical part most organizations miss: Real experimentation isn't about having an innovation lab or running hackathons. It's about building the capability to:
- Test assumptions quickly and cheaply
- Scale successes rapidly
- Kill failed experiments without blame

Fundamental #4: Deep Redundancy

Deep redundancy transcends traditional approaches to organizational backup and recovery systems. Organizations often believe that having disaster recovery plans at the board level and maintaining backup systems at the C-suite level creates resilience. This represents another critical misunderstanding—confusing basic redundancy with true adaptive capability. Real deep redundancy requires boards to maintain multiple strategic options while C-suites build genuinely flexible capabilities. Understanding how this operates at both governance and execution levels reveals why traditional approaches fail to create true resilience.

Consider how TSMC (Taiwan Semiconductor Manufacturing Company) approaches redundancy. They don't just have backup power systems or spare parts. They've built what they call "multiple virtual fabs" - the ability to shift production between facilities seamlessly. But here's what makes it deep redundancy:
- Skills are cross-trained across locations
- Knowledge is distributed, not centralized
- Capabilities are replicated, not just resources

When China threatened Taiwan in 2022, TSMC wasn't just relying on physical backup plans - they had deep capability redundancy that meant they could maintain operations under almost any scenario.

THE FUNDAMENTALS OF RESILIENT ORGANIZATIONS

Compare that to how Colonial Pipeline handled their 2021 ransomware attack. They had traditional backup systems, but lacked deep redundancy in their:
- Decision-making capabilities
- Operational knowledge
- Customer communication systems

The result? A six-day shutdown that triggered fuel shortages across the Eastern United States.

Fundamental #5: Cultural Coherence

Cultural coherence is the fundamental that ties everything together, but it's also the one most organizations get spectacularly wrong at both levels. Boards think cultural coherence means approving value statements, while C-suites think it means enforcing them. Both miss the point. Real cultural coherence requires boards to set cultural direction while empowering C-suites to build it. Let me show you what this governance-execution partnership looks like.

When Satya Nadella transformed Microsoft's culture, he didn't just write new value statements. He rewired how the entire organization:
- Thought about success
- Approached failure
- Made decisions
- Worked together

The result wasn't just better performance - it was true resilience. When COVID-19 hit, Microsoft didn't need new crisis plans. Their coherent culture meant teams could:
- Adapt quickly without central direction
- Innovate within clear boundaries
- Support each other across silos

But here's the warning: Cultural coherence isn't about everyone thinking alike. It's about having a shared understanding of:
- How we make decisions

- What we value
- How we handle challenges
- Where we're going

Look at how this played out at Netflix. Their famous culture deck isn't just a HR document - it's a blueprint for how the organization functions. When they needed to pivot from DVDs to streaming to content creation, their coherent culture meant they could:
- Make tough decisions quickly
- Reallocate resources without drama
- Maintain focus despite massive change

The Governance-Execution Dynamic

The effective flow of these five fundamentals between board and C-suite creates true organizational resilience, but this integration proves challenging for most organizations. When boards embrace resilient thinking while their C-suites remain trapped in traditional execution models, the organization cannot adapt effectively to disruption. Equally problematic is when C-suites drive adaptation and innovation but find themselves constrained by boards still focused on traditional governance metrics and oversight. This misalignment between governance and execution levels does more than just create inefficiency—it fundamentally undermines an organization's ability to build and maintain true resilience. Whether the disconnect originates at the board or C-suite level, the result is the same: an organization that appears stable during normal operations but proves fragile when facing real disruption.

Look at how Microsoft got this right. Their board didn't just approve Nadella's cloud transformation - they fundamentally changed how they governed. They moved from quarterly metric reviews to capability development oversight. From compliance-focused committees to adaptation-focused governance. They gave Nadella's team clear direction while removing traditional constraints.

The C-suite, in turn, didn't just execute the cloud strategy - they rebuilt Microsoft's operational DNA. This wasn't about implementing board directives. It was about creating new capabilities that the board's direction

THE FUNDAMENTALS OF RESILIENT ORGANIZATIONS

demanded. When COVID hit, this governance-execution alignment meant Microsoft didn't need new crisis plans - they had already built resilience into both levels.

Contrast this with Intel during the same period. Their board maintained traditional governance while their C-suite focused on traditional execution. The result? They lost manufacturing leadership to TSMC and chip design leadership to AMD. Both their board and C-suite were executing perfectly against the wrong future.

This dynamic plays out differently across each fundamental:

In **Adaptive Leadership**, boards must shift from oversight to foresight. Look at how Delta's board empowered Bastian to build capabilities before COVID hit. They didn't just approve his plans - they changed their governance model to enable true adaptation.

With **Network-Centric Operations**, resilient boards create governance networks while C-suites build operational ones. P&G's board doesn't just review innovation metrics - they've rebuilt their entire governance structure around network capabilities.

For **Rapid Experimentation**, boards must move beyond risk management to capability building. Amazon's board doesn't just monitor AWS experiments - they've made experimentation part of their governance model. This empowers their C-suite to build true experimental capability.

Deep Redundancy requires boards to maintain strategic options while C-suites build operational flexibility. TSMC's board doesn't just review contingency plans - they govern multiple possible futures. This enables their C-suite to build true redundancy, not just backup systems.

Cultural Coherence flows from governance values to operational reality. When Microsoft's board shifted from compliance to adaptation, it gave Nadella's team permission to rebuild Microsoft's culture from the ground up.

The key is that resilience can't be delegated. Boards can't just tell C-suites to "become resilient" any more than C-suites can build resilience without board support. True resilience emerges when governance and execution evolve together

Putting the Fundamentals into Action

Implementing these fundamentals requires profound organizational transformation that goes far beyond typical change management initiatives. A comprehensive McKinsey study released in 2021 of over 2,000 organizations found that transformations fail about 70% of the time; and building resilience is transformation. Organizations often make the critical mistake of treating this as another project to be managed—assigning it to transformation teams, hiring consultants to create frameworks, or establishing program offices to track metrics. They very often end up doubling down on processes that are either the antithesis of resilience, create false assurances of success, or both. This approach fundamentally misunderstands what building true resilience requires. The integration of these fundamentals demands a complete rewiring of organizational DNA, affecting every aspect of how the organization thinks, operates, and adapts. It requires sustained commitment at both governance and execution levels, fundamentally changing how boards direct strategy and how C-suites implement it. Organizations that succeed in this transformation don't simply modify their processes or update their structures—they fundamentally alter how they understand and respond to challenges at every level. The experiences of organizations that have successfully navigated this transformation offer crucial insights into this complex but essential journey.

Start Where You Are

When Anne Mulcahy took over a nearly bankrupt Xerox in 2001, she didn't try to implement all five fundamentals at once. She started with what was most critical: adaptive leadership. Here's her exact sequence:

1. First 30 Days:
- Met with employees at all levels
- Identified key decision points that needed to be pushed down

THE FUNDAMENTALS OF RESILIENT ORGANIZATIONS

- Started breaking down information silos

2. First Quarter:
- Rebuilt decision-making processes
- Created rapid feedback loops
- Empowered front-line managers

3. First Year:
- Developed network capabilities
- Built experimentation protocols
- Started deepening redundancies

But here's what made it work - she didn't treat it like a transformation program. She treated it like survival.

The story of Mulcahy's transformation of Xerox shows us something crucial about implementing fundamentals - it's not about perfect sequence, it's about survival instinct. When she gathered her leadership team in that first week, she didn't present a transformation roadmap. Instead, she told them a hard truth: 'We have enough cash for a year. That's it.' This created the urgency that drove everything else. It wasn't about checking boxes or following best practices. It was about building new muscles before the old ones gave out. This survival-driven approach changed how everyone viewed the work ahead

The Three Critical Shifts

To implement these fundamentals, you need to make three shifts in your organization:

1. From Programs to Capabilities

Look at how Adobe shifted from selling software packages to cloud-based subscriptions. They didn't just change their business model - they built new capabilities:
- Continuous customer feedback

- Rapid feature development
- Dynamic resource allocation

2. From Control to Enablement

When Microsoft moved to cloud services, they had to shift from controlling every aspect of their software to enabling others to build on their platform. This meant:
- New partnership models
- Different security approaches
- Changed success metrics

3. From Planning to Sensing

Consider what happened during the Apollo 13 mission. When the oxygen tank exploded, success didn't come from following a predetermined plan - no one had planned for that specific failure. Instead, it came from NASA's built-in capability to sense problems and adapt solutions in real-time. The team didn't need permission to innovate; they had already built that capability. This same principle shaped how NASA operates today. Rather than trying to predict every possible problem, they've built systems that can detect and respond to the unexpected. NASA's modern approach to space missions shows this perfectly. Instead of trying to plan for every contingency, they build:
- Real-time monitoring systems
- Adaptive decision protocols
- Distributed problem-solving capabilities

Making Resilience Real: Implementation Challenges

Most organizations struggle with implementation in the crucial early stages of building resilience. Traditional approaches often create an environment where acknowledging problems becomes professionally dangerous, leading to hidden issues that eventually emerge as major crises. Ford's transformation under Alan Mulally demonstrates how this challenge can be overcome. Within his first month, Mulally established

THE FUNDAMENTALS OF RESILIENT ORGANIZATIONS

weekly business plan reviews where executives used a simple red/yellow/green status reporting system. The pivotal moment came when an executive reported a "red" status for the first time. Instead of punishment or criticism, Mulally applauded—creating instant cultural permission for honest problem identification. This response demonstrated how leadership behavior, not formal programs, transforms organizational culture and enables true resilience.

The difference between successful and failed implementations often lies in how organizations interpret what building resilience requires. While successful transformations focus on fundamental behavioral and cultural change, most organizations fall into predictable traps that undermine their efforts. These implementation challenges persist not because they're unavoidable, but because organizations keep approaching resilience-building through traditional change management mindsets. Understanding these pitfalls and challenges, and how they manifest in real organizations, reveals why so many resilience efforts fail despite genuine commitment and substantial resources.

Common Pitfall #1: The Program Trap

The Program Trap represents perhaps the most common implementation failure. Organizations instinctively reach for familiar tools when attempting to build resilience, defaulting to traditional change management approaches. They create formal programs, launch training initiatives, and redesign processes—all while missing the fundamental transformation required for true resilience. These efforts often appear comprehensive on paper, measuring activities and tracking completions, yet fail to create any real adaptive capability.

Most organizations try to implement these fundamentals through:
- Change management programs
- Training initiatives
- Process redesigns

General Electric's failure under Jeff Immelt perfectly illustrates this trap. Despite launching dozens of transformation initiatives, including their much-publicized $4 billion digital transformation program, GE never achieved the fundamental rewiring needed for true resilience. Each new program added complexity without building capability, eventually contributing to a 75% decline in market value between 2016 and 2019.

Microsoft under Satya Nadella showed how to avoid this trap by:
- Starting with real work challenges
- Making changes in how actual decisions were made
- Building capabilities through daily operations
- Integrating resilience into core functions
- Transforming how the organization worked

This wasn't about running parallel change initiatives—it was about transforming how the organization functioned at its core

Common Pitfall #2: The Metrics Mirage

The Metrics Mirage represents another critical implementation challenge. Organizations often believe they're building resilience by tracking and improving traditional performance metrics, mistaking better numbers for better capability. This focus on measurable indicators rather than underlying organizational capacity creates a dangerous illusion of progress, leading organizations to celebrate improved metrics while actually becoming more fragile. When Best Buy was fighting for survival against Amazon, they could have fallen into this trap by focusing on traditional metrics like:
- Store performance
- Cost reduction
- Inventory turns

Instead, CEO Hubert Joly focused on building capabilities:
- Employee engagement
- Customer problem-solving
- Digital integration

The result? Best Buy didn't just survive - they built true resilience that's still paying off today. Best Buy's transformation under Joly illustrates perhaps the most important lesson about implementing fundamentals -

THE FUNDAMENTALS OF RESILIENT ORGANIZATIONS

the difference between activity and capability. While competitors were launching digital initiatives and innovation labs, Joly was rebuilding how the organization functioned at its core. He understood that resilience isn't a program you run; it's a capability you build. This distinction would prove crucial when COVID-19 hit, and Best Buy adapted to curbside pickup in just 48 hours. They didn't need to create new processes - they had already built the capability to adapt.

Common Pitfall #3: Ignoring Warning Signs

Organizations often fail to recognize when their resilience transformation begins to falter. Like a slow leak in a tire, the degradation of resilience efforts typically happens gradually, with subtle signs appearing long before serious problems emerge. This erosion frequently begins despite maintaining apparent progress on surface-level metrics or completing designated transformation activities. The warning signs appear across multiple dimensions of the organization, from how decisions are made to how information flows. Understanding these indicators enables leaders to intervene before their resilience efforts completely derail. Here are the early indicators that signal a transformation losing momentum:

1. Return to Old Metrics:
- Focus shifts back to purely financial measures
- Short-term targets dominate discussions
- Innovation metrics get ignored

2. Decision Regression:
- Decisions move back up the hierarchy
- Response times slow down
- Risk tolerance decreases

3. Cultural Drift:
- Silos start reforming
- Information sharing decreases
- Blame culture reemerges

Common Challenge #1: Measuring Progress Without Killing Momentum

Building resilience requires measuring progress, yet the very act of measurement can undermine the transformation itself. Organizations must track their evolution, but traditional metrics often drive behavior back toward linear thinking and away from true resilience. Even successful leaders frequently derail their transformation efforts by defaulting to familiar measurement approaches that emphasize control over capability development. The challenge lies in finding ways to measure progress that reinforce rather than inhibit resilience-building. Starbucks provides an instructive example of how organizations can approach this challenge.

They don't just track:
- Store performance
- Revenue growth
- Customer satisfaction

Instead, they measure:
- How quickly stores can adapt to new customer needs
- How effectively knowledge spreads across the network
- How many innovations come from front-line employees

Common Challenge #2: Picking Metrics That Matter

The metrics an organization chooses to track reveal much about their understanding of resilience. Traditional measurements focus on outcomes and static performance indicators, while true resilience metrics must capture an organization's capacity for adaptation and evolution. The difference isn't just in what gets measured, but in how those measurements inform organizational development. Microsoft's approach to tracking their transformation demonstrates how organizations can select metrics that actually indicate growing resilience rather than just improved performance.

THE FUNDAMENTALS OF RESILIENT ORGANIZATIONS

1. Adaptive Capability Metrics:
- Time from problem identification to solution implementation
- Number of decisions made at lower levels
- Speed of resource reallocation

2. Network Effectiveness:
- Cross-functional collaboration frequency
- Information flow speed
- Problem-solving across boundaries

3. Experimentation Impact:
- Learning cycle time
- Innovation adoption rates
- Failed experiment insights captured

These measurements serve as indicators of growing organizational capability, not just numbers on a dashboard. They reveal how effectively the organization is building the systemic capacity to adapt and evolve.

Common Challenge #3: Maintaining Momentum

Starting organizational transformation generates natural energy and enthusiasm, but maintaining momentum over time presents a far greater challenge. Organizations typically navigate the first few months of change effectively, driven by initial excitement and clear short-term goals. However, sustaining true transformation requires systematic approaches that embed new behaviors and capabilities into the organization's daily operations. This challenge becomes particularly acute when early successes create the temptation to relax transformation efforts. Adobe's evolution from packaged software to cloud services demonstrates how organizations can systematically maintain momentum through structured yet flexible approaches to embedding change.

1. Regular Reality Checks:
- Monthly capability assessments
- Quarterly direction adjustments

- Annual strategy evolution

2. Continuous Learning Loops:
- Weekly team retrospectives
- Monthly cross-functional reviews
- Quarterly organization-wide learning sessions

3. Leadership Alignment:
- Daily operational synchronization
- Weekly strategic adjustments
- Monthly capability reviews

The Long Game: Ensuring Sustainable Resilience

The contrast between Intel and AMD provides a compelling illustration of how sustainable resilience actually works in practice. In 2015, Intel dominated chip manufacturing with what looked like unassailable advantages:
- Manufacturing excellence
- Massive scale
- Deep R&D capabilities

But they fell into what I call the "capability trap" - they got so good at what they did, they couldn't change how they did it. By 2021, they'd lost their manufacturing edge to TSMC and their design leadership to AMD.

Now look at how AMD approached resilience under Lisa Su's leadership:
- Separated design from manufacturing
- Built flexible partnerships
- Focused on capability development over asset ownership

The result? AMD went from near-bankruptcy to outperforming Intel in both innovation and market value.

Making It Stick

THE FUNDAMENTALS OF RESILIENT ORGANIZATIONS

Resilience is not going to happen because those in positions of influence and authority say it will. Rather, there are three key aspects the organization needs to understand to ensure resilience efforts have a shot at sticking. Each aspect requires both governance and execution levels to evolve not just their actions, but their fundamental approach to building lasting capability. Let me show you exactly how this works in practice.

1. Understanding and approaching the distinction between the board and C-suite's roles in resilience development

Let me show you exactly how this distinction plays out in practice. When Anne Mulcahy stepped into the CEO role at Xerox, she faced what looked like a clear division of labor: the board would govern, and she would execute. But that traditional distinction nearly killed their transformation. It wasn't until both levels fundamentally reimagined their roles that real resilience emerged.

The board realized that their job wasn't just to monitor performance metrics – it was to actively shape how the organization would build future capabilities. Meanwhile, Mulcahy understood that her role wasn't just to execute board directives – it was to create the mechanisms for ongoing adaptation. This dual transformation changed everything.

Board Level:
- Sets long-term capability requirements
- Evaluates succession through resilience lens
- Maintains strategic continuity while enabling adaptation

C-Suite Level:
- Rotates leaders through different roles
- Develops decision-making capabilities
- Builds systematic innovation skills

Look at how Microsoft implements this dual-level approach:

Their board:

- Evaluates executive succession based on adaptation capability
- Reviews strategic initiatives through resilience lens
- Maintains clear resilience expectations across leadership changes

Their C-suite:
- Rotates leaders across cloud, AI, and traditional products
- Develops adaptive decision-making at every level
- Builds innovation capabilities through systematic exposure to new challenges

This isn't just about division of responsibilities – it's about creating a resilience engine that works at both levels. When Microsoft faced the mobile revolution's disruption under Ballmer, they had the same governance-execution split they'd always had. But it wasn't working. Under Nadella, they rebuilt not just what each level did, but how they worked together to sense and respond to change.

The key lesson? Resilience isn't built through clear division of labor – it's built through clear division of purpose. The board shapes the capability agenda while the C-suite creates the mechanisms to deliver it. When both levels understand this distinction, true resilience becomes possible.

2. Cultural Reinforcement

Consider what happened at Microsoft in 2014. Their culture was so broken that employees spent more time competing with each other than with competitors. They had values statements, cultural initiatives, and leadership principles – all the standard corporate culture tools. But none of it mattered because their board saw culture as a C-suite problem, while their C-suite saw it as an HR initiative.

The transformation started when Microsoft's board realized something crucial: cultural resilience isn't a program to monitor – it's a capability to govern. Meanwhile, Nadella understood that his role wasn't to write new value statements but to rewire how the organization functioned at its core. This dual-level approach to culture changed everything.

THE FUNDAMENTALS OF RESILIENT ORGANIZATIONS

Building and reinforcing resilient culture across governance and execution:

Board Level:
- Sets cultural resilience expectations
- Evaluates cultural health beyond metrics
- Maintains cultural continuity through change

C-Suite Level:
- Implements cultural transformation initiatives
- Develops cultural adaptation capabilities
- Builds systematic cultural reinforcement

Look at how Salesforce implements this dual-level approach:

Their board:
- Mandates investment in cultural development
- Reviews cultural initiatives through resilience lens
- Maintains clear cultural expectations across transitions

Their C-suite:
- Drives innovation through regular hackathons
- Creates customer co-creation opportunities
- Builds continuous learning into operations
- Rewards cultural adaptation behaviors

The contrast with Intel during the same period is telling. Their board treated culture as a C-suite responsibility, while their C-suite treated it as a series of programs. The result? Despite billions in resources and market leadership, they couldn't adapt to fundamental market shifts. Their culture became their constraint precisely because neither level understood how to build cultural resilience.

The message is clear: Cultural resilience isn't built through programs or initiatives. It's built through a fundamental partnership between governance and execution, where boards actively shape cultural capability while C-suites create the mechanisms to develop it. When both levels align on this approach, culture becomes a source of resilience rather than resistance.

3. Integrating resilience across organizational systems and operations

Real system-wide resilience emerges when organizations fundamentally transform their entire operating model. When P&G decided to transform their innovation model, they could have treated it as a series of isolated changes. Instead, they did something remarkable — they rebuilt their entire operating system from board governance through frontline execution. The result was their "Connect + Develop" model that didn't just change how they innovated; it changed how the entire organization functioned.

But here's what most people miss about P&G's transformation: It worked because both their board and C-suite understood that systems integration isn't about connecting processes — it's about building capability at every level. This wasn't a top-down mandate or a bottom-up initiative. It was a complete rewiring of how the organization sensed, decided, and acted.

Board Level:
- Approves system-wide resilience investments
- Reviews integration progress quarterly
- Ensures long-term system sustainability

C-Suite Level:
- Leads operational system transformation
- Develops cross-functional capabilities
- Builds integrated response mechanisms

Look at how Adobe implements this dual-level approach:

Their board:
- Approved comprehensive cloud transition
- Mandated customer-centric system integration

THE FUNDAMENTALS OF RESILIENT ORGANIZATIONS

- Maintained strategic focus through transformation

Their C-suite:
- Rebuilt entire product development process
- Transformed customer engagement systems
- Created new pricing and delivery models
- Integrated resilience across all operations

If we consider the earlier discussion of Kodak, we can see an instructive contrast. Kodak's board approved digital initiatives while their C-suite launched digital projects, but neither level understood that true systems integration requires rebuilding the organization's fundamental capabilities. They had digital programs but not digital DNA. They had innovation initiatives but not innovative capability. The result? A company that invented digital photography couldn't survive the digital transformation.

This pattern – of treating systems integration as a series of connected programs rather than a capability-building imperative – repeats across failed transformations. The winners, like Adobe, understand that resilient systems aren't just connected – they're capable. They don't just share information; they build collective capability.

The Three Questions Every Leader Must Answer

Before we wrap up this chapter, you need to honestly answer these questions:
1. Are you building metrics or capabilities?
2. Is your organization actually becoming more adaptive?
3. Can your resilience outlast your leadership?

Because here's the brutal truth: The next disruption isn't going to wait for your transformation program to finish. You need to build resilience while running your business, just like changing a jet engine mid-flight.

In the next chapter, we'll explore exactly how to start your resilience journey. But remember - this isn't about survival. It's about building an organization that gets stronger with every challenge it faces.

4

STARTING YOUR RESILIENCE JOURNEY

Building organizational resilience requires fundamental changes at both governance and execution levels. While many organizations recognize this need, their approaches to transformation often differ dramatically, leading to starkly different outcomes. Understanding these differences—and why they matter—requires examining how organizations approach resilience-building at both board and C-suite levels. Two organizations in the same industry, facing identical challenges, demonstrate how different approaches to transformation create vastly different results.

In 2019, both CVS Health and Rite Aid faced the same challenge. Both boards recognized the need for healthcare transformation. Both C-suites had similar resources, comparable store networks, and faced the same market pressures. But their governance and execution approaches couldn't have been more different.

CVS took what looked like a crazy risk - investing billions in healthcare capabilities while competitors focused on traditional pharmacy operations. They:

- Acquired Aetna for $69 billion
- Transformed stores into healthcare hubs
- Built new capabilities in virtual care

When COVID-19 hit, they didn't just survive - they became central to the nation's healthcare response. Meanwhile, Rite Aid struggled through another restructuring.

The difference? CVS didn't start with a transformation program. They started with a fundamental question: "What capabilities do we need to matter in the future?"

Aligning Governance and Execution from Day One

Let's think about professional sports for a moment. When the team takes to the pitch or the F1 driver pulls onto the starting grid, they all have one thing in common, they are already on the same page as their coach, team staff, pit crew, etc. They have a shot at winning, because between them, strategy and execution are in planned alignment. While not always obvious as we watch a player sink a goal, or our driver take the checkered flag, the genesis for that moment began before the event started. Yet this basic concept is what derails so many organizations when they start their resilience journey. Most fail before they begin because they don't align board direction with C-suite capability building. They either have boards demanding resilience without enabling it, or C-suites trying to build it without governance support.

Look at how Best Buy got this right under Hubert Joly. Before any transformation began, their board made three critical moves:

- Shifted from quarterly performance oversight to capability development
    - Created new governance committees focused on adaptation
    - Changed how they measured executive success

This gave Joly's team the strategic freedom to rebuild Best Buy's DNA. They didn't have to fight governance to build resilience - governance demanded it. When Amazon's threat intensified, Best Buy didn't need board approval for radical changes - they'd already built the governance-execution alignment to move fast.

Contrast this with Toys "R" Us's final transformation attempt. Their board maintained traditional governance while demanding digital transformation. Their C-suite tried building new capabilities while being measured on old metrics. The result? Bankruptcy, because you can't build resilience when governance and execution are misaligned.

This alignment challenge shows up in every major turnaround:
- Nokia's board demanded mobile innovation while maintaining PC-era governance
- BlackBerry's board wanted digital transformation while measuring quarterly device sales

STARTING YOUR RESILIENCE JOURNEY

- Blockbuster's board asked for streaming capability while governing for store metrics

The survivors approach it differently:
- Microsoft's board rebuilt governance before Nadella began transformation
- Adobe's board changed oversight models before their cloud transition
- Delta's board shifted metrics before Bastian built crisis resilience

Here's what this means for your journey: Before you launch any transformation program, get crystal clear on the governance-execution alignment.

Your board needs to:
- Rewrite their oversight approach
- Rebuild committee structures
- Revise success metrics
- Reset stakeholder expectations

Your C-suite needs to:
- Design capability-building plans
- Create transformation roadmaps
- Build new operational models
- Develop talent strategies

Most importantly, both levels need to move in lockstep. Resilience isn't built through governance dictates or execution heroics. It emerges when both levels evolve together toward a resilient future

Starting Right: The First 30 Days

Breaking from the linear mindset that resilience development is a only project within a larger set of organizational tasks, we need to look at resilience as a journey, in order to be successful in its execution. This means that when as a leader, you are planning how to develop your organizational resilience, you do not start with a steering committee or a consultant's assessment. It starts with three critical steps that most organizations get wrong.

Step 1: Reality Check
Not your market analysis or SWOT assessments. It's about brutal honesty at both levels:
Board Level Reality:
- What strategic capabilities you oversee (not what you assume exists)
- Where your governance approach blocks change
- Whether your oversight truly enables resilience

C-Suite Level Reality:
- What operational capabilities you have (not what you claim)
- Where your organization resists change
- What your culture actually values (not what's on the posters or CEO emails)

Look at how Satya Nadella started Microsoft's transformation. His first move wasn't announcing a new strategy. It was admitting Microsoft had lost its way and needed to fundamentally change how it operated.

Step 2: Capability Mapping
Most organizations start with restructuring or process changes. That's exactly backwards. Let me show you how Amazon approaches this.
When Amazon decided to enter healthcare, they didn't start by buying hospitals or hiring doctors. They mapped their existing capabilities:
- Logistics excellence
- Customer data analytics
- Technology infrastructure
- Innovation processes

Then they mapped what they needed:
- Healthcare expertise
- Regulatory compliance capabilities
- Medical supply chain knowledge

STARTING YOUR RESILIENCE JOURNEY

- Patient care delivery systems

The gap between these maps became their transformation roadmap.

Step 3: Quick Wins That Matter
Here's where most organizations go wrong - they chase quick wins that look good but build no real capability. Let me show you the difference.

When General Motors started their electric vehicle transformation, they could have:
- Launched a few EV models
- Created some green initiatives
- Made sustainability announcements

Instead, they:
- Built battery development capabilities
- Created new supplier networks
- Developed software expertise
- Transformed manufacturing processes

The difference? The first list produces metrics. The second builds resilience.

The First 90 Days: Building Momentum

Now we're getting to the hard part - moving from planning to actual change. And this is where most organizations stall in their efforts; they got off to a good start but failed to sustain the momentum beyond the initial feel-good segments. Losing momentum is why so many organizational efforts obtain the distinction of joining the "initiative of the quarter" club. Let's learn from a successful effort, in how Microsoft sustained momentum under Nadella:

Days 1-30:
- Started "live site" reviews where problems were discussed openly
- Eliminated stack ranking of employees
- Launched listening tours across all divisions

Days 31-60:
- Initiated cross-functional teams
- Started cloud transformation
- Began restructuring incentives

Days 61-90:
- Launched first major partnership initiatives
- Started cultural transformation programs
- Initiated new innovation processes

Scaling What Works: The Next Level

Let me show you where most organizations stumble after their initial successes. They try to scale by:
- Creating more programs
- Adding more metrics
- Rolling out more initiatives

That's exactly how GE failed under Jeff Immelt. Instead, look at how JP Morgan Chase built their digital transformation:

They didn't just:
- Launch digital products
- Create innovation labs
- Hire tech talent

They systematically built new capabilities:
- Created internal technology academies.
- Embedded engineers in business units.
- Built cross-functional product teams.

The difference? One approach creates activities. The other builds lasting capability.

Common Pitfalls and How to Avoid Them

STARTING YOUR RESILIENCE JOURNEY

Organizations attempting to build resilience often stumble in predictable ways, not because the path is unclear, but because they default to familiar approaches that undermine true transformation. These failures typically emerge early in the process, when initial enthusiasm meets organizational reality. Understanding where and why these initiatives typically falter enables leaders to recognize and avoid common traps that can derail even well-intentioned efforts. The patterns of failure reveal themselves consistently across industries and organization types:

Pitfall 1: The Metrics Trap

Wells Fargo fell into this one hard. They measured:
- New accounts opened
- Products per customer
- Sales targets

We all know how that ended. Instead, look at how Capital One approaches metrics:
- Customer problem resolution speed
- Innovation adoption rates
- Cross-team collaboration effectiveness

Pitfall 2: The Program Syndrome

Remember Radio Shack's last transformation attempt? They:
- Launched multiple initiatives
- Created transformation offices
- Rolled out training programs

Compare that to Best Buy's approach under Hubert Joly:
- Built real capabilities in digital commerce
- Developed new customer service models
- Created flexible store formats

One company doesn't exist anymore. The other thrived through disruption.

Maintaining Momentum: The Long Game

Here's where even successful transformations often fail - they lose steam after initial wins. Let me show you how the real winners maintain momentum.

Look at how Microsoft keeps their transformation going:

1. Regular Reality Checks

Not just performance reviews, but hard looks at:
- Emerging market shifts
- New competitor capabilities
- Internal resistance points

2. Capability Building Cycles

They don't just train people - they:
- Rotate leaders through different roles
- Create deliberate learning experiences
- Build new skills through real projects

3. Cultural Reinforcement

This isn't about posters and values statements. They:
- Celebrate learning from failures
- Reward cross-boundary collaboration
- Promote based on capability building

The Warning Signs

Early indicators of failing resilience initiatives often appear well before major problems emerge. These signals, drawn from organizations across industries, consistently precede significant deterioration in transformation efforts. Recognizing these warnings enables leaders to intervene before their resilience-building efforts collapse completely. Based on extensive analysis of organizational transformations, several critical indicators reliably predict impending failure:

STARTING YOUR RESILIENCE JOURNEY

1. Return to Old Patterns

- Decisions start moving back up the hierarchy
- Risk-taking decreases
- Innovation slows down

Look at what happened to Yahoo. After initial transformation success, they slid back into:

- Centralized decision making
- Risk aversion
- Slow innovation cycles

2. Capability Erosion

- Cross-functional collaboration decreases
- Learning cycles slow down
- Information sharing diminishes

This is exactly what killed Kodak - not their failure to see digital coming, but their erosion of adaptive capabilities.

Wrapping It Up

The stories of Microsoft, CVS, Best Buy, and others we've explored aren't just transformation tales - they're proof that real resilience is possible even in the face of massive disruption. But they also demonstrate something more important: resilience isn't a destination, it's an ongoing evolution.

Look at Apple today. They've moved from computers to mobile devices to wearables to services. Each shift required new capabilities, different ways of operating, fresh approaches to markets. Yet through it all, they've maintained their core ability to adapt and evolve. That's not accident or luck - it's engineered resilience.

Toyota's decades-long journey shows us that true resilience gets stronger with each challenge. Their production system didn't just survive disruptions - it improved because of them. Every problem became a learning opportunity, every setback sparked innovation, every challenge built new capability.

The leaders who understand this don't just survive disruption - they use it as fuel for growth. They recognize that today's capabilities, no matter how strong, are just a foundation for building tomorrow's. They know that resilience isn't about having perfect plans or bulletproof systems - it's about building organizations that get stronger through change.

The organizations that thrive in the decades ahead won't be the ones with the best plans or the strongest current market positions. They'll be the ones that have built the capability to adapt, learn, and emerge stronger from whatever challenges arise.

This isn't about predicting the future. It's about building organizations that can shape it.

5

RESILIENCE IN THE AGE OF GENERATIVE AI

Despite decades of anticipation and extensive analysis of AI's potential impact, many organizations proved surprisingly unprepared for its emergence as a disruptive force. The contrast became clear in November 2022 when OpenAI released ChatGPT. Two leading financial institutions demonstrated markedly different approaches at both governance and execution levels. JP Morgan Chase's board defaulted to traditional risk oversight, leading their C-suite to restrict access, citing security concerns. Goldman Sachs' board, meanwhile, provided strategic direction for AI transformation, empowering their C-suite to move quickly on integration, with CEO David Solomon executing on what the board declared a key strategic priority. These contrasting governance-execution approaches defined each organization's AI resilience journey.

By mid-2023, the contrast was clear. JP Morgan had to reverse course, with Jamie Dimon admitting in his annual letter to shareholders that AI would "dramatically impact" their industry and announcing plans to deploy 300 AI use cases. Goldman Sachs was already using AI to enhance everything from trading to client interactions, having built what Solomon called "a collaboration between human capital and AI."

The Real AI Disruption

Let's be clear about something: The rise of Generative AI isn't just another tech trend. McKinsey estimates it could add $4.4 trillion in annual value to the global economy. But here's what most leaders miss - this isn't about the technology. Generative AI is not the first time new technology has disrupted traditional organizations. From the steam engine's transformation of manufacturing in the 1700s through the assembly line's reshaping of production in the early 1900s, to computers revolutionizing

information processing by mid-century, and mobile phones connecting the world in the 1990s, technological disruption has consistently reshaped how organizations operate and compete. What Generative AI is about is actually a reminder, not something new, of how disruption forces organizations to rethink everything:
- How work gets done
- What creates value
- Where human expertise matters
- How organizations learn and adapt

Look at Microsoft's approach. Their board didn't just approve a $13 billion OpenAI investment - they set a comprehensive AI resilience strategy. At the governance level, they:
- Mandated organization-wide AI transformation
- Set clear ethical boundaries for AI development
- Established long-term AI capability requirements

Their C-Suite then executed by transforming:
- Product development processes
- Customer support systems
- Software testing approaches
- Employee training and development

This alignment between board direction and C-suite execution enabled Microsoft to build true AI resilience, demonstrated through rapid integration of AI capabilities across their entire product ecosystem. Unlike competitors who treated AI as just another technology initiative, Microsoft's approach created systemic capability for continuous AI evolution and adaptation. The results speak clearly: within eighteen months, Microsoft integrated AI functionality across their product suite while maintaining ethical standards and building sustainable competitive advantage.

The New Rules of AI Oversight

RESILIENCE IN THE AGE OF GENERATIVE AI

Let me show you why traditional technology governance fails with AI. Most organizations try to govern AI like they governed previous tech transformations - through risk committees, compliance frameworks, and capability reviews. That's exactly why they're failing.

Look at what happened at major banks in 2023. Their boards tried governing AI through traditional technology oversight committees. Their risk frameworks treated AI like any other tech implementation. Their governance processes demanded certainty in an inherently uncertain domain. The result? They fell months behind while more adaptively governed competitors moved forward.

The winners approached it differently. Microsoft's board didn't just create an AI oversight committee - they fundamentally rewired how they governed technology:

Old Tech Governance They Abandoned:
- Quarterly capability reviews
- Traditional risk frameworks
- Project-based oversight
- Compliance-focused monitoring

New AI Governance They Built:
- Continuous capability evolution
- Adaptive risk frameworks
- Ecosystem-based oversight
- Ethics-focused governance

This new governance model gave their C-suite the freedom to build true AI resilience. They weren't constrained by traditional oversight - they were empowered by adaptive governance.

Compare that to Meta's struggle. Their board maintained traditional tech governance while pouring $27 billion into AI. Their C-suite tried building AI capabilities while being measured by traditional metrics. The result? They fell behind smaller, more adaptively governed competitors.

The pattern is clear: Organizations that govern AI like traditional technology fail. Those that build new governance models thrive. Look at how NVIDIA's board approaches AI:

- They don't just review AI projects - they assess AI ecosystem development.
- They don't just monitor AI risks - they govern AI evolution.
- They don't just track AI metrics - they measure AI capability building.

This governance model lets their C-suite move at AI speed. When generative AI exploded in late 2022, NVIDIA didn't need new governance approval - they had already built the oversight structure for rapid adaptation.

The message is clear: AI resilience requires new rules at both levels. Boards can't govern AI through traditional frameworks any more than C-suites can build AI capabilities through traditional processes. Both must evolve together to create true AI resilience.

The Capability Gap

Look at what happened to IBM in 2023. Despite having Watson and decades of AI experience, they found themselves scrambling to catch up with Microsoft and Google in generative AI capabilities. Their stock dropped 9% in a single day when CEO Arvind Krishna admitted they'd fallen behind. This wasn't a technology problem - it was a resilience failure.

Compare that to NVIDIA's approach. Jensen Huang didn't just ride the AI wave - he spent years building the capabilities needed to lead it:
- Developed specialized AI chips before the market existed
- Built comprehensive developer tools and ecosystems
- Created training programs for AI engineers
- Established partnerships across the tech industry

The result? When generative AI exploded, NVIDIA's market value soared past $1 trillion because they had built true resilience through capability development.

The Integration Challenge

Microsoft's success with AI isn't just about their OpenAI partnership. Looking at how they're actually implementing AI across their organization, we see what are arguably, at least at this stage of AI, best practices for establishing resilience around AI:

1. Capability Building:

- Created AI training programs for all employees
- Established AI centers of excellence
- Built cross-functional AI implementation teams
- Developed new AI governance frameworks

2. Process Integration:

- Redesigned software development workflows
- Created new quality assurance methods
- Established AI ethics review boards
- Built new security protocols

3. Cultural Adaptation:

- Shifted from code ownership to prompt engineering
- Developed new collaboration models
- Created AI experimentation frameworks
- Established clear AI use guidelines

What we see from this is Microsoft's approach to AI success goes beyond external partnerships, demonstrating a holistic integration across capability building, process refinement, and cultural transformation – a fundamental approach to any effort that drives resilience. By embedding AI into across their organization's ecosystem—through training, governance, workflow redesign, and cultural adaptation—they're setting a powerful precedent for how large organizations can leverage AI to drive innovation and ensure sustainable growth.

The Reality of AI Integration

Look at Walmart's approach to AI resilience. In 2023, they didn't just announce AI initiatives - they fundamentally rewired their operations. They:
- Acquired five AI companies including Getit Technologies.
- Built an AI tool that automates over 65,000 routing queries daily.
- Transformed their supply chain with predictive analytics.
- Retrained 50,000 employees in AI capabilities.

Compare that to Target's more hesitant approach. While they've implemented some AI in inventory management, their slower adoption has led to them playing catch-up in areas like:
- Personalized customer experiences
- Supply chain optimization
- Employee productivity tools
- Automated decision-making

The Talent Reality

Even well-intentioned companies often miscalculate when adapting to disruptive technologies like AI. Consider Google's misstep in 2023: after laying off 12,000 employees, they found themselves scrambling to rehire AI talent just months later. This case exemplifies a common misunderstanding—AI doesn't merely eliminate jobs; it reshapes them, creating demand for entirely new skillsets and capabilities.

Contrast this with Morgan Stanley under James Gorman's leadership, which serves as a model of thoughtful adaptation. Instead of seeing AI as a threat to their workforce, they embraced it as a partner in transforming roles and processes. Their approach was deliberate and multifaceted:

- AI-Powered Research Platform: They launched a robust platform, now serving 70,000 clients, that synthesizes data at speeds unattainable by human analysts alone.

- AI Assistants for Advisors: By creating AI tools to streamline decision-making, they enhanced—not replaced—the capabilities of financial advisors.

- AI-Enhanced Risk Assessment Tools: New systems improved their ability to evaluate complex risk scenarios with unprecedented precision.

- Upskilling and Integration: They invested heavily in retraining employees, ensuring their existing workforce could collaborate seamlessly with AI systems.

This strategy wasn't about replacing people; it was about transforming how they work. By prioritizing integration over disruption, Morgan Stanley aligned technology with human expertise, demonstrating what true resilience looks like in the age of AI. What we take away from this is that organizations that treat AI as a replacement tool risk creating capability gaps and operational instability – that is, they reduce resilience. Those that see it as a force multiplier, enhancing human potential, position themselves to thrive in disruption.

The Security Imperative

Samsung learned this lesson the hard way in April 2023, when employees leaked sensitive code through ChatGPT, revealing failures at both governance and execution levels. Contrast this with Microsoft's dual-level approach to AI security.

Board Level:
- Established AI governance frameworks
- Set clear risk tolerance boundaries
- Mandated comprehensive security protocols
- Required regular security compliance reviews

C-Suite Level
- Built enterprise-grade safety features
- Implemented clear usage guidelines
- Developed technical security measures
- Created incident response protocols

The difference? Microsoft's board owned the governance while empowering their C-suite to own the execution.

Building Real AI Resilience

Adobe's 2023 transformation around AI wasn't just a technological upgrade; it was a deliberate strategy to build resilience into their core operations and culture. Rather than react to disruptions like Midjourney and Stable Diffusion, Adobe created systems and processes to thrive amid uncertainty. Here's how they did it:

- Future-Proofed Ecosystem: By embedding their Firefly AI across all products, Adobe didn't just add features—they created a unified ecosystem designed to evolve with user needs.
- Trust as a Differentiator: They launched robust content authenticity protocols to address growing concerns about AI-generated misinformation, positioning themselves as a trusted leader.
- Customer Empowerment: Through comprehensive AI training programs, they equipped their users with the skills to adapt alongside the technology, fostering long-term loyalty and collaboration.
- Agile Business Models: New pricing structures for AI-enhanced tools allowed Adobe to align its revenue streams with rapid technological changes, reducing dependency on traditional revenue models.

The key to Adobe's success wasn't just innovation—it was the foresight to prioritize adaptability over perfection. By fostering a culture of experimentation and creating systems designed to evolve, Adobe became an exemplar of AI resilience. Their journey highlights a fundamental truth: resilience isn't just surviving disruption—it's shaping it.

The Hard Realities

Meta's challenges in 2023 illustrate the consequences of focusing on investment rather than capability. Despite pouring $27 billion into AI research, they failed to keep pace with OpenAI. The reason? Meta concentrated on advancing technology instead of embedding AI resilience into their organization.

Microsoft, under Satya Nadella, provides a stark contrast. By combining a $13 billion OpenAI partnership with systemic change, they transformed how AI integrates into their operations:
- AI capabilities embedded across product lines
- AI-enhanced workplace tools redefining productivity
- Comprehensive employee training programs for working alongside AI
- Clear, actionable AI ethics guidelines

The key difference? Microsoft didn't just adopt AI—they reshaped their business to thrive in an AI-driven world. Their resilience strategy focused on building scalable capabilities, enabling adaptation to both anticipated and unexpected challenges.

The Cost of Hesitation

2023 demonstrated how hesitating to adapt to AI innovation left traditional banks scrambling. Fintech disruptors like Stripe and Square harnessed AI to revolutionize operations:
- Automated underwriting streamlined approvals
- Real-time fraud detection cut response times to seconds
- Personalized financial services enhanced customer engagement
- Predictive cash flow analysis offered businesses unprecedented foresight

In contrast, banks like Wells Fargo and Citigroup were caught flat-footed. The issue wasn't resources but resilience—they lacked the organizational flexibility to pivot quickly. Fintech companies thrived because they built systems capable of rapid iteration, proving that hesitation is the antithesis of resilience.

The Implementation Reality

Salesforce's 2024 strategy highlights the difference between adding AI features and cultivating resilience. Guided by Marc Benioff, Salesforce created a framework designed for agility and sustainability:
- Einstein AI was seamlessly integrated across their platform
- AI-powered predictive analytics became foundational to decision-making
- AI training certifications empowered clients and employees alike
- Ethical AI governance frameworks ensured trustworthiness

When OpenAI's advancements disrupted the market, Salesforce adapted with confidence. Their success stemmed from embedding adaptive capability into their DNA, enabling them to integrate new AI developments without disruption. Resilience wasn't an afterthought—it was their strategy.

The Trust Factor

Anthropic's response to competition from OpenAI and Google in late 2023 demonstrates the critical role trust plays in resilience. Instead of focusing solely on technical superiority, they addressed enterprise concerns with deliberate actions:
- Detailed safety protocols reinforced reliability
- Ethical guidelines were established to align AI use with values
- Monitoring systems ensured operational transparency
- Transparent incident response processes-built client confidence

This trust-centric approach transformed their competitive position. Anthropic's actions show that resilience isn't just technical—it's about building systems that ensure stakeholders' trust even in volatile environments

The Market Reality

IBM's stock drop in October 2023 wasn't about missing quarterly goals—it reflected their failure to adapt to the AI era. Without flexible AI capabilities, robust partnerships, or a culture of rapid iteration, they were outpaced by competitors.

- Meanwhile, Microsoft's market value exceeded $3 trillion. Their resilience was built on:
  - Dynamic AI integration processes, enabling swift adaptation
  - Strategic partnerships that reinforced innovation
  - Governance frameworks ensuring ethical and scalable AI use
  - Holistic employee training to maximize AI potential

The lesson? Markets reward organizations that prepare for transformation rather than react to it

The Human Element

Amazon's launch of the Q AI assistant for AWS in late 2023 was impressive—but what ensured its success was the groundwork laid beforehand:

- Technical teams across the company were retrained to operate in an AI-first environment.
- AI development protocols were revamped to accelerate innovation.
- Guidelines for ethical and effective AI use were codified across divisions.
- AI ethics review boards were established to oversee operations and ensure alignment with organizational values.

Amazon's strategy underscores a critical truth: technology can only go as far as the people using it. By prioritizing human capability alongside technical advancement, they ensured resilience in an industry defined by rapid change

Measuring What Matters

In 2024, organizations that excel at AI resilience are redefining what success looks like. Microsoft's approach exemplifies the shift from tracking traditional implementation metrics to measuring the systems and behaviors that drive resilience.

Traditional Metrics They Abandoned:
- Number of AI models deployed
- AI features launched
- AI tools implemented

What They Measure Instead:
- Speed of AI Integration: How quickly AI capabilities enhance product performance and customer experience
- Employee AI Capability Development: Progress in upskilling employees to leverage AI effectively
- AI Solution Adaptation Rates: How quickly existing AI tools evolve in response to user feedback and market demands
- Cross-Functional AI Collaboration: The extent and efficiency of AI-related teamwork across departments

Microsoft's focus demonstrates that resilience isn't about hitting arbitrary numbers—it's about enabling continuous improvement, agility, and alignment across the organization

The Competitive Landscape

By January 2024, the market started showing clear winners and losers in AI adaptation. Look at the enterprise software space:
Snowflake:
- Launched Cortex AI capabilities
- Built AI-powered data optimization
- Created new AI governance tools
- Developed AI integration frameworks

Oracle:
- Struggled to match competitors' AI capabilities
- Played catch-up in AI integration
- Failed to build comprehensive AI training
- Lagged in AI governance development

The stock market's response was brutal, but it wasn't about the technology - it was about organizational resilience to implement and adapt to AI changes.

The Real Winners and Losers

The winners in the AI era aren't those with the biggest budgets or the most advanced individual tools. They are the ones that avoid the trap of linear thinking and plan for resilience by embedding adaptability into their systems, culture, and strategies.

Take NVIDIA as a case in point. While others in the tech industry treated AI as a feature set to roll out, NVIDIA anticipated how AI would redefine their entire market. They didn't focus solely on building better GPUs; instead, they transformed themselves into the backbone of AI innovation. Here's how:

- Diversification of Capabilities: NVIDIA invested in hardware, software, and ecosystems, ensuring they could deliver end-to-end AI solutions rather than just components.
- Strategic Partnerships: They built deep collaborations with companies like OpenAI, enabling them to stay ahead of technological trends while creating demand for their platforms.
- Scalable Adaptation: By fostering a culture of experimentation, NVIDIA was able to rapidly iterate and integrate new AI breakthroughs into their products and services.

Their success wasn't the result of perfect forecasting—it was the result of building systems that allowed them to adapt to and shape the AI revolution.

Contrast this with IBM, which struggled in 2023 despite its history of innovation. While NVIDIA focused on resilience by aligning their strategy with AI's transformational potential, IBM clung to linear thinking, focusing on incremental improvements and outdated success metrics. Their reliance on short-term wins and isolated initiatives left them unprepared for the scale and speed of AI-driven disruption.

The lesson from this is that linear thinking assumes today's achievements will seamlessly carry organizations into tomorrow's success. It prioritizes deliverables over capabilities and reacts to disruption instead of anticipating it.

Resilient organizations like NVIDIA take a different approach:

- Building Capability Ecosystems: They don't just focus on tools or products; they create integrated systems designed to evolve.

- Leveraging Collaboration: Partnerships and open ecosystems allow them to share risks, accelerate innovation, and stay ahead of emerging trends.

- Scaling Adaptation: They prepare not for specific disruptions but for the ability to respond to any disruption, ensuring agility becomes a competitive advantage.

The choice is clear. Organizations that cling to linear thinking will find themselves outpaced by those that build resilience into their core. The real winners aren't just reacting to the AI era—they're shaping it.

The Hard Lessons

Resilience doesn't happen by accident—it requires intentionality, alignment, and foresight. Yet even well-resourced organizations can struggle when they treat resilience as a checkbox exercise rather than an embedded capability. A critical lesson from successful organizations is that ad hoc strategies, reactive governance, and unclear frameworks only amplify the challenges of disruption.

One of the most damaging traps is linear thinking: assuming today's successes can be directly extended into tomorrow's challenges without systemic change. Leaders who fail to prioritize adaptability over rigid systems often find their organizations unable to navigate complexities like AI integration, compliance, or cross-functional alignment.

The case of Goldman Sachs in 2023 is a stark example of how linear thinking undermines resilience. While CEO David Solomon championed AI adoption early on, the organization fell into a familiar pattern of fragmented implementation:

- Their internal AI tool for developers had limited adoption

- Legal teams restricted AI use due to compliance concerns
- Teams struggled with data privacy in AI implementation
- Shadow AI use increased despite official policies

Compare that to Morgan Stanley's more systematic approach under Ted Pick:
- Built clear AI governance frameworks
- Created comprehensive data privacy protocols
- Developed specific use cases for each division
- Established training programs at all levels

The difference? Morgan Stanley didn't treat AI as a technological project but as a strategic transformation requiring systemic alignment. By embedding resilience into their AI strategy, they not only avoided disruptions but also accelerated adoption and innovation.

The lesson for leaders is clear: without systems designed to adapt, even the best intentions can lead to missed opportunities and increased risks. Building resilience isn't about avoiding disruption—it's about anticipating it and ensuring your organization is ready to thrive when it happens

The Market Reality Check

By early 2024, the winners and losers of the AI era were becoming increasingly clear. Companies like Microsoft, Salesforce, and Amazon stood out, not just because they implemented AI effectively but because they built the organizational systems to support it. Microsoft's 300% productivity increase, Salesforce's 40% faster customer issue resolution, and Amazon's 50% reduction in product development time weren't just numbers—they were the results of deliberate strategies to align people, processes, and technology.

In contrast, companies like IBM, SAP, and Oracle struggled to keep pace. Despite their resources, these organizations fell behind because they approached AI as a technology challenge rather than a systemic transformation. They missed critical opportunities to integrate AI into workflows, align governance with execution, and equip their people to adapt. The result was predictable: missed targets, lost market share, and a growing sense of irrelevance.

What separated the winners from the losers wasn't just speed or budget—it was their ability to recognize that AI, like any major disruption, demands more than surface-level adjustments. Organizations that succeeded embraced resilience as a core capability, building systems designed to adapt and evolve as the environment changed.

Lessons from Success and Failure

Take Microsoft's rapid deployment of Copilot across its ecosystem. While some might focus on their technological achievements, the real story lies in how they built the systems to support it: cross-functional collaboration, scalable governance, and workforce training that reached every level of the organization. These efforts allowed Microsoft to not just implement AI but integrate it meaningfully, turning disruption into opportunity.

In contrast, Oracle's sluggish AI rollout highlighted the pitfalls of treating technology adoption as an isolated task. Without governance in place or an adaptable culture, Oracle lost valuable time and market share, leaving them struggling to keep up with more adaptive competitors.

Similarly, NVIDIA's transformation under Jensen Huang demonstrated how cultural adaptation fuels resilience. By ensuring their entire workforce became AI-fluent and embedding collaboration and ethics into their operations, NVIDIA positioned itself as a leader in the AI era. Compare this to Intel, which limited AI access to specialized teams and delayed governance frameworks, maintaining traditional structures ill-suited for rapid change. The result? NVIDIA emerged as an innovator, while Intel found itself falling behind.

Even success stories faced challenges. Organizations like Adobe and Salesforce thrived not because they avoided obstacles but because they anticipated and addressed them. Adobe's Firefly rollout succeeded not just because of its innovative features but because of the groundwork laid in advance: user training, clear timelines, and systems for rapid feedback. Salesforce's ability to embed AI into customer workflows stemmed from listening to users and aligning AI capabilities with real-world needs.

Key Success Lessons:
- Cross-Functional Collaboration: Microsoft's alignment of teams across governance and execution allowed for rapid deployment and scalable innovation.
- Cultural Adaptation: NVIDIA fostered AI fluency at all levels, embedding adaptability into their organizational DNA.
- Proactive Planning: Adobe anticipated challenges and addressed them with training, timelines, and systems for feedback.
- Customer-Centric Innovation: Salesforce aligned AI capabilities with user workflows and needs, driving adoption and impact.

Key Failure Lessons:
- Siloed Governance: Oracle's lack of integrated governance and cultural adaptability led to slow adoption and lost market share.
- Restrictive Access: Intel's limited AI access and delayed governance stifled agility and collaboration.
- Short-Term Thinking: Organizations that treated AI adoption as a one-off task failed to create systems for sustained innovation.

The difference between success and failure lies not in resources but in mindset. Resilient organizations focus on systems, adaptability, and long-term capability, turning disruption into an opportunity to lead.

Resilience as the Connecting Thread

The lessons from these successes and failures aren't limited to AI—they reflect the broader principles of resilience that underpin this book. Whether the challenge is a global pandemic, supply chain disruptions, or the rapid emergence of generative AI, the organizations that thrive share a common trait: they don't just react to change; they plan for it.

Resilient organizations think beyond short-term metrics. They align governance and execution, ensuring that strategy informs operations and vice versa. They invest in capabilities—whether technological, cultural, or structural—that enable them to adapt to disruptions they can't yet predict. Most importantly, they recognize that resilience isn't a destination; it's a practice, a mindset embedded in every layer of the organization.

As this chapter demonstrates, the AI era is just the latest proving ground for resilience. The same principles that helped organizations navigate past disruptions apply here: systems that adapt, cultures that foster collaboration, and leaders who understand that resilience is about more than surviving disruption—it's about using it as a springboard for growth.

When viewed through this lens, the AI revolution isn't just a challenge; it's an opportunity to build the kind of resilience that will define the next generation of organizational success.

6

SELECTING AND PROMOTING RESILIENT LEADERS

In 2015, two leadership transitions unfolded in the tech world, each with very different outcomes. Satya Nadella stepped into the CEO role at Microsoft, inheriting a company with strong finances but a fragile foundation for future growth. At Intel, Brian Krzanich was chosen as CEO based on traditional metrics—stock performance, revenue growth, and operational efficiency in their manufacturing operations.

Fast forward to 2024, and the contrast couldn't be more striking. Under Nadella's leadership, Microsoft's value increased by over $2 trillion, cementing its place as a resilient and adaptive industry leader. Meanwhile, Intel has cycled through three CEOs—Krzanich, Bob Swan, and Pat Gelsinger—while losing manufacturing leadership to TSMC and chip design leadership to AMD, despite having both the resources and talent to maintain their market position.

The difference between these two organizations wasn't experience or expertise. Both companies had deep technical knowledge, strong market positions, and ample resources. What set them apart was their capacity for resilient leadership—a forward-thinking approach that prioritizes adaptability, innovation, and long-term sustainability over short-term wins.

Let's break down what resilient leadership truly looks like in practice and why it has become the defining trait of successful organizations in an era of constant disruption.

The Leadership Selection Problem

Look at what happened at Boeing. Their board selection process failed at two critical levels:

Board Selection Failures:

- Chose directors focused on financial oversight alone
- Selected members prioritizing quarterly returns
- Maintained traditional governance approaches

C-Suite Selection Failures:
- Picked executives focused on short-term metrics
- Promoted leaders resistant to transformation
- Selected operators over adaptors

This two-level failure in leadership selection created a perfect storm – a board unable to direct resilience selecting C-suite leaders unable to build it.

The result? A culture that put metric achievement above safety, leading to the 737 MAX crisis and a fundamental breakdown in organizational resilience.

Compare that to how Jeff Bezos selected his successor at Amazon. He didn't just look for:
- Strong operational performance
- Financial acumen
- Industry expertise
- Management experience

Instead, he sought someone who could:
- Build new capabilities
- Adapt to changing markets
- Foster innovation
- Maintain cultural resilience

Selecting leaders who can build true organizational resilience requires confronting some deeply uncomfortable truths about how most organizations evaluate and choose their leaders.

The Hard Truth About Leadership Selection

SELECTING AND PROMOTING RESILIENT LEADERS

Look at Intel's decline in semiconductor leadership. Their board selected leaders who were great at running the existing business. They chose safe bets - executives who:
- Had strong track records in operations
- Showed consistent financial performance
- Knew the industry inside and out
- Maintained strong relationships

And that's exactly why they lost their competitive edge to TSMC and Samsung. They picked leaders who could execute yesterday's playbook when they needed leaders who could write tomorrow's.

The Leadership Reality Check

Here's what you need to understand: If your current leaders can't build resilience, they're not just failing to move you forward - they're actively making you vulnerable. This isn't about being nice. It's about survival.

Look at what happened at Nokia. They had brilliant leaders who:
- Hit their numbers
- Managed costs effectively
- Maintained market share
- Met board expectations

And they drove the company straight into irrelevance because they couldn't adapt to disruption.

The Non-Negotiables

When selecting leaders, certain criteria prove essential for building organizational resilience. While specific requirements differ between board and C-suite levels, core capabilities must exist at both levels. The evidence is clear and uncompromising: leaders lacking these fundamental qualities not only fail to build resilience—they actively undermine it.

Organizations serious about survival must make the hard choice to replace such leaders, regardless of their other qualifications or past successes. It is not lost on me the need for a sense of loyalty within organizations — this is a notable aspect called out in many studies as a key to retaining critical talent; but, if at the end of the day your resilience effort roadblocks or challenges keep aligning to the same people, you're only hurting the larger organization by not taking, unpleasant but needed, action. The requirements are non-negotiable:

Board Director Requirements:
1. Strategic Adaptation
- Not: 'Let's maintain current oversight'
- But: 'Let's rethink governance for resilience'
2. Risk Direction
- Not: 'Let's avoid all risks'
- But: 'Let's set clear risk parameters for transformation'
3. Governance Evolution
- Not: 'I've served on many boards'
- But: 'Traditional governance must evolve'

C-Suite Requirements:
1. Operational Adaptation
- Not: 'We've always done it this way'
- But: 'Let's build new capabilities'
2. Risk Intelligence
- Not: 'Let's study this for six months'
- But: 'Let's test this now and learn quickly'
3. Learning Agility
- Not: 'I have 20 years of experience'
- But: 'Everything we know might be obsolete tomorrow"

Let's look at what happened when organizations had the courage to make tough leadership calls - and when they didn't.

The Cost of Hesitation

Look at Boeing again. Boeing's failure with Dennis Muilenburg as CEO represents perhaps the starkest example of hesitation's devastating cost. By 2018, clear warning signs emerged that Muilenburg's leadership actively undermined organizational resilience. Despite his strong financial performance—Boeing's stock had doubled under his tenure—the board had mounting evidence that his approach was creating systemic vulnerability. Muilenburg's decisions consistently prioritized short-term market performance over Boeing's long-standing commitment to engineering excellence and safety culture.

Their board knew Dennis Muilenburg wasn't building resilience. They saw:
- Focus on stock price over safety
- Emphasis on short-term metrics over long-term capability
- Resistance to organizational change
- Defensive responses to problems

As for taking action…they waited. And waited. The cost of that hesitation? 346 lives lost.

Everything else - the $20 billion in costs, the destroyed public trust, the crippled organizational culture - while significant for business, pales in comparison to the human cost this fundamental failure of leadership enabled.

The Contrast

Microsoft's board demonstrates how to handle leadership that undermines resilience. By 2013, Steve Ballmer's limitations had become clear. Despite Microsoft's continued profitability, Ballmer had missed mobile computing entirely, actively resisted cloud transformation, maintained outdated power structures, and watched competitors innovate while Microsoft stagnated. The company's market value remained flat for fourteen years under his leadership, even as the tech sector boomed. During his tenure, in the face of tech sector disruption from new technology and competition, rather than providing Microsoft with resilience, Ballmer enabled:

- Dismissed iPhone as having "no chance" of gaining market share, then spent $7.2 billion on Nokia only after missing the mobile revolution.

- Actively resisted cloud computing transformation until Amazon had established dominant market position.

- Maintained a destructive stack-ranking culture that pitted employees against each other, stifling innovation and collaboration.
- Clung to Windows-first strategy even as the market shifted to mobile and cloud platforms.
- Lost nearly half of Microsoft's market value while competitors like Apple and Google saw exponential growth during the same period.

They acted. They didn't wait for a crisis; they did not wait for Microsoft to take further hits due to a CEO who could not develop resilience against competitor-driven disruption. They saw where the trend was heading, and didn't wait for metrics to crash. They brought Satya Nadella onboard.

The Warning Signs

Here are the non-negotiable red flags that signal a leader needs to go:

1. Metric Obsession
- Focuses on numbers over capabilities
- Celebrates hitting targets while missing market shifts
- Rewards compliance over innovation
- Values predictability over adaptability

2. Change Resistance
- Defends current practices
- Dismisses emerging threats
- Delays difficult decisions
- Defaults to past solutions

3. Cultural Stagnation
- Surrounds themselves with yes-people
- Punishes bad news
- Maintains power hierarchies
- Resists new perspectives

Making the Tough Calls

SELECTING AND PROMOTING RESILIENT LEADERS

Resilient leadership is about more than just finding someone with a track record of success—it's about finding someone who can align the organization's capabilities with the disruptions and opportunities that lie ahead. Hiring a leader who excels at maintaining the status quo may bring short-term stability, but it's a recipe for long-term vulnerability.

This principle was powerfully illustrated in the 2011 film *Margin Call*. In a pivotal moment, the CEO (played by Jeremy Irons) explains, "I'm here for one reason and one reason alone. I'm here to guess what the music might do a week, a month, a year from now. That's it. Nothing more." This sentiment encapsulates the essence of resilience-focused leadership: the ability to anticipate and prepare for what's coming, not just optimize for what is.

When Best Buy's board selected Hubert Joly as CEO in 2012, critics and analysts declared the decision a mistake. Joly wasn't a retail insider, a tech expert, or even a proven CEO. In fact, he represented everything the industry considered risky in leadership selection. But Joly brought something far more important: a willingness to rebuild the company's capabilities and reimagine its culture.

Under Joly's leadership, Best Buy underwent a radical transformation:
- Cultural Adaptation: He reinvigorated a struggling workforce by focusing on employee development, customer experience, and shared purpose.
- Capability Building: Joly invested in e-commerce and digital integration, creating a competitive edge against online juggernauts like Amazon.
- Adaptation to Change: Rather than trying to "out-Amazon" Amazon, Joly doubled down on what Best Buy could do best: providing expert advice, customer service, and in-store experiences.

The result was remarkable. Best Buy not only survived but thrived in a retail environment dominated by Amazon, becoming a case study in how bold, forward-thinking leadership can build resilience.

In contrast, consider GE's struggles under successive leaders in the 2010s. GE often prioritized leaders who were deeply rooted in its traditional operations, focused on incremental improvements rather than anticipating industry shifts. As a result, the company failed to adapt to seismic changes in energy, healthcare, and industrial automation. By selecting leaders tied to the past rather than the future, GE's resilience steadily eroded.

Why Resilience Requires Forward-Looking Leadership

Resilience isn't about optimizing for today's conditions—it's about preparing for tomorrow's disruptions. Boards and C-suites must shift their mindset when selecting leaders, prioritizing those who:
- Understand the forces reshaping the industry
- Are willing to challenge the status quo and rebuild capabilities
- Can foster adaptability in culture, operations, and strategy
- Have the courage to take risks and reimagine what success looks like

A 2023 study by McKinsey reinforces this point: companies that appoint leaders with experience in navigating disruptions—whether in other industries or complex environments—are 35% more likely to outperform peers during times of transformation.

The lesson for boards is clear. Resilient organizations are built by leaders who understand that their role isn't just to maintain the music—it's to anticipate its next movement and prepare the organization to thrive, no matter what comes next.

The Execution Reality

Let's be brutally honest: resilience demands more than just plans and strategies—it requires leadership that actively drives transformation. If your organization has leaders who:
- Hide behind metrics instead of addressing root issues,
- Avoid tough decisions when they are clearly necessary,
- Cling to the status quo as disruption accelerates,
- Resist real, meaningful change,

then it's time for them to go. Not next quarter. Not after the next review cycle. Now.

SELECTING AND PROMOTING RESILIENT LEADERS

The hardest part isn't recognizing the problem; it's acting on it. Organizations often confuse a hard decision—acknowledging that a leader is holding back resilience—with the hard conversation required to make that decision a reality. No one enjoys delivering difficult news, but mistaking discomfort for deliberation can paralyze the organization.

Consider what happened at GE during Jeff Immelt's tenure. The signs of stagnation were clear:
- Market value dropped by $500 billion
- Digital transformation initiatives failed to gain traction
- Innovation slowed to a crawl
- The company's culture became rigid and resistant to change

And yet, Immelt stayed in his position far too long because he checked enough traditional boxes to justify it. Stockholders and board members clung to metrics that looked good on the surface, despite clear evidence that GE's resilience was eroding. This wasn't just a leadership failure—it was an organizational failure to make the tough decision to prioritize future growth over current comfort.

The Lesson for Leaders

If resilience is the goal, organizations must stop rationalizing poor leadership fit. A leader's inability to enable change is not a gap to manage—it's a risk to mitigate. The true cost of keeping someone who resists resilience isn't just stagnation; it's the opportunity cost of the adaptability, innovation, and momentum your organization loses every day they stay.

This isn't about being ruthless; it's about being resolute. By separating the emotional challenge of the conversation from the strategic necessity of the decision, organizations can take the steps needed to position themselves for future success. Building resilience requires leaders who don't just accept disruption but embrace it. If someone can't—or won't—align with that vision, they don't belong in the room.

The Selection Imperative

Choosing leaders who can enable resilience isn't just about filling a role—it's about ensuring the organization can thrive in an environment of continuous disruption. Resilient organizations look beyond traditional leadership qualifications and focus on capabilities that drive adaptability, transformation, and growth. Here's what that means in practice:

1. Adaptability Over Experience
- Not: "20 years in the industry."
- But: "20 examples of driving change."

A 2021 study by McKinsey found that companies with leaders who prioritize adaptability are 24% more likely to outperform peers during market disruptions. Experience is valuable, but only if it comes with a demonstrated ability to pivot, innovate, and manage through uncertainty. Adaptability ensures leaders can navigate not just the current landscape but the unpredictable challenges ahead.

2. Learning Over Knowing
- Not: "I have all the answers."
- But: "I know how to find better questions."

Research from the Center for Creative Leadership highlights that learning agility—the ability to continuously acquire and apply new knowledge—is one of the strongest predictors of leadership success. Leaders who embrace a growth mindset are better equipped to challenge assumptions, reframe problems, and uncover new opportunities.

3. Building Over Maintaining
- Not: "I can run this business."
- But: "I can transform this business."

A 2020 Deloitte survey of global executives revealed that organizations undergoing transformation significantly outperform their competitors when they prioritize leaders who focus on building future-ready capabilities over maintaining existing operations. Leaders who can drive systemic change and reimagine business models are essential for long-term resilience.

Why This Matters

Selecting leaders based on traditional metrics—like tenure or familiarity with the status quo—does little to prepare organizations for the future. In an era defined by rapid disruption and complexity, boards and decision-makers must shift their focus toward identifying individuals who thrive in uncertainty, embrace change, and inspire innovation. The data is clear: leaders with these traits are far better equipped to drive resilience, ensuring their organizations are positioned not just to survive disruption, but to capitalize on it.

This mindset shift also requires broadening the search for leadership talent. The right leaders to build resilience might not come from within your industry—and that's a good thing. Resilience isn't about industry-specific expertise; it's about adaptability, creativity, and the ability to reimagine what's possible. A leader who has transformed a technology company might be just as capable of helping a shoemaking organization adapt to supply chain disruptions or shifting consumer behaviors. Narrowing the pool to only those who have "been in the trenches" of a specific sector risks reinforcing the very status quo you're trying to overcome.

Resilience-focused organizations know that the best leaders bring a fresh perspective, a willingness to challenge assumptions, and the skills to build systems capable of evolving. The question isn't whether they've made shoes before—it's whether they can build a shoemaking organization that's ready for the next disruption.

The Real Implementation

At JP Morgan Chase, leadership selection for 2024 and beyond reflects a seismic shift in how resilience is prioritized. Traditional metrics like revenue responsibility, team size, years of experience, and industry knowledge are no longer the focal points. Instead, their new criteria demand clear, measurable evidence of leadership traits that align with future needs:

- Successfully Navigating Disruption: Leaders must demonstrate how they have steered their organizations through complex and volatile challenges. According to a 2021 McKinsey study, companies led by disruption-ready executives were 30% more likely to outperform peers during industry shifts.
- Building New Organizational Capabilities: Beyond maintaining operations, these leaders must have a proven ability to create new frameworks, tools, or systems to future-proof their organizations.
- Transforming Existing Operations: Evidence of turning outdated processes or structures into engines of growth is non-negotiable.
- Developing Resilient Teams: Resilience isn't just about the individual leader—it's about their ability to empower and adapt their teams to face uncertainty.

The Selection Process

Microsoft provides an excellent case study in how to implement resilience-focused leader selection. By shifting from traditional methods to innovative, future-focused criteria, they've ensured their leadership aligns with the company's long-term goals.

Old Process They Abandoned:
- Performance Reviews: Focused on past metrics, not future adaptability
- Succession Planning Charts: Static tools that failed to account for rapidly evolving needs
- Skills Assessments: Emphasized existing abilities over growth potential
- Behavioral Interviews: Useful for cultural fit but insufficient for resilience-building

New Process They Implemented:
- Disruption Response Scenarios: Leaders must prove their ability to think on their feet during simulated crises.

SELECTING AND PROMOTING RESILIENT LEADERS

- Innovation Track Record: Past achievements in driving meaningful innovation are now essential.
- Capability Building History: Evidence of establishing systems or tools that enable sustainable growth.
- Cultural Transformation Evidence: A leader's ability to reshape and align an organization's culture is a critical differentiator.

This shift reflects broader research. A Deloitte 2022 study found that organizations prioritizing leadership adaptability saw 35% greater innovation output and were 20% more likely to sustain growth through disruption.

Embracing Hard Decisions

Pat Gelsinger's rapid impact at Intel showcases the importance of decisiveness in leadership restructuring. Within 90 days of becoming CEO, Gelsinger made sweeping changes to reposition Intel for resilience:
- Replaced 11 Senior Executives: Recognizing that the old guard lacked the mindset to drive change, he swiftly brought in fresh leadership.
- Restructured Leadership Teams: Breaking down silos, Gelsinger ensured alignment across the organization.
- Rebuilt Reporting Structures: Simplifying how information flowed allowed for faster decision-making.
- Revamped Incentive Systems: By aligning rewards with resilience-building outcomes, he reinforced the right behaviors.

These moves demonstrated a key principle: maintaining existing leadership often means maintaining existing limitations. Leaders must align with the future, not the comfort of continuity.

The Promotion Reality

Promotion practices can either drive resilience or undermine it. Many organizations fall into the trap of promoting leaders based on:
- Current Performance: A snapshot of today, not a measure of tomorrow's potential

- Technical Expertise: Necessary, but insufficient for broader organizational impact
- Time in Role: Longevity doesn't equate to leadership for resilience
- Political Relationships: Favoritism over fitness for the future

Amazon, by contrast, evaluates leadership potential with a forward-focused lens:
- Ability to Build New Capabilities: Demonstrating how they've constructed tools, systems, or teams for long-term success
- Track Record of Driving Adaptation: Evidence of embracing and thriving during change
- Fostering Innovation: A proven ability to inspire and implement transformative ideas
- Developing Resilient Teams: Leaders who create adaptable, engaged, and future-ready teams

Research from the Harvard Business Review supports this approach, finding that leaders who foster adaptability and innovation are 32% more likely to deliver sustained organizational performance.

The Transition Reality

Leadership transitions can define an organization's future. Here are three examples that highlight what works—and what doesn't:

Success Story: Microsoft
When Satya Nadella took over, he didn't just shift strategy—he redefined leadership practices:
- Eliminated Stack Ranking: Ending a toxic system that discouraged collaboration
- Rebuilt Incentive Systems: Aligning rewards with behaviors that foster resilience
- Transformed Decision-Making Processes: Empowering teams with autonomy and speed
- Rewired the Culture: Creating an environment that prioritized learning and experimentation

Result: A $2.8 trillion market valuation and a leadership position in AI transformation.

Failure Story: Intel
Between 2013 and 2021, Intel clung to outdated leadership models:

- Promoted leaders based on tenure, not adaptability
- Maintained rigid hierarchies that stifled innovation
- Used traditional metrics that failed to capture future needs
- Protected power structures over capability development

Result: Lost manufacturing leadership to TSMC and design dominance to AMD.

Redemption Story: AMD
Under Lisa Su's leadership, AMD transformed from a struggling company into a market leader:
 - Cleared Out Resistant Leadership: Removing roadblocks to innovation
 - Built New Technical Capabilities: Positioning AMD at the cutting edge
 - Transformed Culture: Encouraging risk-taking and collaboration
 - Rewired Decision-Making Processes: Speeding up how ideas became action

Result: A 1600% stock price increase and a leadership position in critical segments.

The Reality of Selection: Criteria That Build Resilience

The selection of leaders is one of the most consequential decisions an organization makes, yet too often, this process remains rooted in outdated priorities. Many organizations still default to evaluating candidates based on static metrics like:
 - Revenue responsibility

- Size of teams managed
- Years of industry experience
- Familiarity with existing operations

These metrics may identify competent managers, but they rarely surface the kind of leaders who can future-proof an organization. In a rapidly changing landscape, selecting leaders based on the past instead of the future leads to stagnation. Resilience requires more.

Take JP Morgan Chase as an example. In recent years, they've redefined their leadership selection process to focus on qualities that align with long-term adaptability. Their new criteria prioritize:

- Successfully Navigating Disruption: Leaders must demonstrate how they've managed through complex, unpredictable challenges. This doesn't just mean surviving a crisis—it means emerging stronger.
- Building New Capabilities: Evidence of creating new systems, technologies, or processes that position the organization for future success is essential.
- Transforming Existing Operations: Leaders must show they can turn legacy systems and practices into engines of growth.
- Developing Resilient Teams: The ability to build adaptable, forward-thinking teams is a critical marker of leadership that sustains resilience.

This shift reflects what resilience demands: leaders who can thrive amid complexity and guide their teams through the unpredictable.

Moving Beyond Traditional Selection Processes

Microsoft offers another compelling example. Under Satya Nadella's leadership, the company transformed its selection processes, abandoning traditional tools like:

- Performance Reviews: These often focus on past accomplishments rather than future potential.
- Succession Planning Charts: Static charts can't adapt to dynamic organizational needs.
- Skills Assessments: Valuable but insufficient when they fail to measure resilience-building capabilities.

SELECTING AND PROMOTING RESILIENT LEADERS

- Behavioral Interviews: Useful for cultural fit but inadequate for evaluating adaptability or innovation.

Instead, Microsoft implemented a forward-focused selection process emphasizing:
- Disruption Response Scenarios: Leaders are evaluated on how they would navigate high-pressure, rapidly changing situations.
- Innovation Track Records: Past achievements in introducing meaningful change are now essential.
- Capability-Building Evidence: A demonstrated history of developing systems, processes, or teams that enable long-term resilience.
- Cultural Transformation Leadership: The ability to foster collaboration, openness, and adaptability across teams and divisions.
- This approach ensures that the leaders Microsoft selects are aligned with the company's long-term vision and resilient to ongoing disruption.

What Happens When Selection Goes Wrong

Failure to align leadership selection with resilience can have devastating consequences. GE's struggle under Jeff Immelt offers a cautionary tale. Despite his strong traditional metrics—revenue growth, market dominance, and tenure—Immelt's leadership failed to anticipate the digital transformation required for the company's future. By sticking with the wrong leader for too long, GE suffered:
- A $500 billion decline in market value
- Failed digital transformation initiatives
- Stagnating innovation
- A rigid, calcified culture

Immelt's example underscores a fundamental truth: selecting leaders based on outdated metrics isn't just a mistake—it's a risk to the organization's survival.

Defining Resilience-Focused Selection Criteria

Resilient organizations redefine what they look for in leaders. Instead of prioritizing the past, they focus on qualities that drive future success. The most effective selection criteria include:

- Adaptability in Uncertainty: Can this leader thrive when the ground shifts beneath them? Have they demonstrated an ability to pivot and guide teams through disruption?

- Capacity to Build and Rebuild: Has this leader built systems, teams, or processes that position an organization for sustained growth?

- Cultural Leadership: Can this leader align teams, foster innovation, and create a culture of adaptability?

- Forward-Looking Vision: Does this leader see what's coming next, and do they have the courage to act on it before others do?

Resilience-focused selection isn't about finding the best candidate for the job as it is today—it's about finding the right leader for what the organization needs to become.

When Lisa Su took over at AMD, she embodied these principles of resilience-focused leadership. Su didn't just manage AMD—she transformed it. She:

- Cleared out resistant leadership, replacing those who clung to old ways.

- Built new technical capabilities, aligning AMD with future market opportunities.

- Rewired company culture to embrace collaboration and risk-taking.

- Introduced processes that enabled faster, more adaptable decision-making.

Rebuilding The Selection Process Itself

Even great organizations fail at leadership selection when they rely on outdated processes. It's like trying to hire an AI expert using a 1990s IT checklist—the process itself undermines the ability to find the leaders who will drive resilience.

SELECTING AND PROMOTING RESILIENT LEADERS

Take Intel between 2015 and 2021. Their board's traditional criteria—industry expertise, public company experience, technical knowledge, and previous board service—produced leaders who executed perfectly against the wrong future. The result? Lost market leadership, missed opportunities, and an erosion of their competitive edge.

Contrast this with Microsoft. They didn't just change selection criteria—they rebuilt the process itself:

- Old Process They Killed: Standard nominating committees, traditional director profiles, conventional interviews, and experience-based evaluations.
- New Process They Built: Capability-focused selection, adaptation-based profiles, scenario-driven evaluations, and future-focused assessments.

This approach brought in directors capable of governing for resilience. These directors then selected Satya Nadella—not because he checked traditional boxes, but because he demonstrated the adaptive capabilities needed to transform Microsoft.

The pattern is clear. Organizations that fail to adapt their selection processes continue to fall behind. Boeing prioritized safety-focused directors but missed broader resilience needs. IBM chose technology-focused leaders but failed to anticipate the cloud revolution. GE picked efficiency-focused directors who couldn't guide transformation.

Winners, like NVIDIA, rebuilt their approach to leadership selection:
- They evaluate adaptation capabilities, not just experience.
- They test future thinking, not just qualifications.
- They assess transformation ability, not just track records.

The takeaway is simple: before you change what you look for in leaders, change how you look for them. Traditional processes produce traditional leaders. Resilient selection processes are the only way to identify leaders who can future-proof your organization.

The New Leadership Criteria

Selecting leaders based on vague or outdated metrics is no longer acceptable. Here's how resilient organizations like Microsoft and Amazon now evaluate candidates:

1. Disruption Response:
Leaders must show evidence of having:
- Led through major disruptions.
- Built new capabilities in challenging contexts.
- Transformed operations to drive sustained change.

2. Learning Agility:
Leaders need a proven ability to:
- Move across functions and industries.
- Lead diverse teams in complex environments.
- Learn from failure and build from scratch.

3. Cultural Impact:
The most effective leaders demonstrate:
- A track record of transforming cultures.
- Experience building resilient, adaptive teams.
- The ability to foster learning and innovation across the organization.

Amazon's leadership process exemplifies these criteria. They demand:
- Documented evidence of building new business models, creating future capabilities, and driving systemic change.
- A proven track record of making tough calls, challenging the status quo, and eliminating sacred cows.
- Clear examples of adapting to disruption, learning from failure, and transforming organizations.

The Hard Implementation Steps

Implementing a resilient leadership standard requires action—not half-measures or gradual transitions. The best organizations act decisively:

1. Clean House:

SELECTING AND PROMOTING RESILIENT LEADERS

Microsoft under Nadella evaluated every senior leader within 30 days. Resistance points were removed, leadership teams were rebuilt, and reporting structures transformed—all in 90 days.

2. Reset Expectations:

AMD under Lisa Su immediately eliminated outdated metrics, created new success criteria, rebuilt incentive systems, and set clear consequences for non-adaptive behaviors.

3. Install Leadership DNA:

NVIDIA demands every leader:
- Build capability
- Drive adaptation
- Foster innovation
- Create resilience
- No exceptions. No compromises

The Reality Check

This section is short and to the point. Organizations more often than note often fail to ensure proper leadership alignment and selection because they prioritize:
- Maintaining relationships
- Protecting feelings
- Avoiding disruption
- Easing transitions

These choices are costly. Consider Boeing, where avoiding tough calls led to:
- Lives lost
- Trust destroyed
- Capability eroded
- Future compromised

Non-Negotiables for Leadership

For any leadership role that is critical to ensuring organizational resilience against disruption, candidates must demonstrate:

- Resilience Building: Clear evidence of creating systems or teams that adapt and thrive.
- Transformation Experience: Proven ability to lead major shifts, not just incremental change.
- Capability Development: A track record of building new skills and frameworks.
- Cultural Impact: Evidence of reshaping and aligning culture with future needs.

The Warning Signs

Here's when you know leaders at either level risk the organization's resilience capability, and need to go:

Board Level Red Flags:
- Focuses solely on quarterly oversight
- Prioritizes compliance over transformation
- Maintains traditional governance models
- Resists evolving strategic direction

C-Suite Level Red Flags:
- Obsesses over operational metrics
- Sacrifices capability for current results
- Maintains outdated processes
- Blocks systematic change

When these warning signs appear at either level, the organization's resilience is actively being compromised. At the board level, it prevents strategic adaptation. At the C-suite level, it blocks capability building. Either one is fatal to resilience.

Wrapping Up: The Hard Truth

SELECTING AND PROMOTING RESILIENT LEADERS

Here's what you need to understand: In today's environment, maintaining non-resilient leadership isn't just risky - it's organizational suicide. Look at the companies that thrived through disruption:

- Microsoft under Nadella
- AMD under Su
- NVIDIA under Huang

What do they have in common? They all made tough leadership calls early, executed quickly, and built true resilience.

The choice is simple but hard: Build resilient leadership now, or become another case study in organizational failure. There's no middle ground, no gentle transition, no comfortable compromise.

The future belongs to organizations led by people who can build resilience, drive adaptation, and create sustainable capability. Everyone else is just managing decline.

Your move.

7

SYSTEMS THINKING AND RESILIENCE

In 2022, Boeing's board reviewed a comprehensive set of safety metrics, risk assessments, and compliance reports. Their C-suite presented detailed plans showing how each measure would improve outcomes. Every box was checked, every metric tracked, every process documented. Yet just months later, the 737 MAX crisis revealed how this linear, checkbox thinking had fundamentally undermined their organization's resilience. What they missed wasn't more metrics or better processes—it was understanding how organizational resilience emerges from the complex interactions between culture, capabilities, processes, and people. Boeing's failure of resilience manifested not just in the 737 MAX crashes—which stemmed from linear, siloed thinking about safety systems—but in their inability to adapt and respond effectively afterward, as their checkbox approach to governance and operations left them without the organizational capability to recognize systemic problems, learn from failures, or rebuild trust with stakeholders. This failure to build resilience wasn't about effort or resources—it arose from a fundamental misunderstanding of how resilient organizations function.

The Boeing case illustrates a fundamental truth about organizational failure: leaders typically focus on the most obvious but least effective points of intervention, optimizing what they can easily measure and control. They adjust metrics, modify processes, reorganize structures, and enhance monitoring—all while missing the deeper reality of how their organization actually works. Instead of seeing their organization as a complex system where every element influences and is influenced by others, they treat it as a collection of independent parts, each to be optimized separately. This reductionist thinking creates the illusion of improvement while actually undermining the organization's ability to function as a cohesive whole, adapt to challenges, or respond effectively to disruption.

Consider Toyota versus General Motors during the 2008-2009 automotive crisis. While GM approached each challenge—inventory, dealer networks, product development—as separate problems to solve, Toyota understood their organization as an integrated system.

Toyota's approach revealed stark differences at both levels:

Board Level:
- Viewed dealer network as part of integrated ecosystem
- Understood how production decisions affected entire supply chain
- Recognized connections between product development and manufacturing
- Measured success through system capability, not just financial metrics
- Built long-term resilience into governance decisions
- Fostered innovation across the entire system

C-Suite Level:
- Created integrated production systems
- Developed adaptive supply chain networks
- Built feedback loops between dealers and manufacturing
- Implemented cross-functional problem solving
- Maintained flexible manufacturing capability
- Measured success through system performance

The results proved stark: When crisis hit, Toyota adapted quickly while GM spiralled into bankruptcy, requiring a $50 billion government bailout to survive. During 2008-2009, GM's sales plunged 30% and they lost $30.9 billion, while Toyota maintained sufficient cash reserves and market stability to acquire market share. Though Toyota's sales also declined, their systemic resilience allowed them to recover faster and emerge stronger—by 2010, Toyota's profit had rebounded to $2.3 billion while GM was still restructuring under government oversight. The difference wasn't resources or market position—it was how they thought about and managed their organization as a system.

This linear thinking failure repeats in industry after industry. Look at how retail transformed under the rise of e-commerce. Sears approached

SYSTEMS THINKING AND RESILIENCE

each challenge—online sales, store operations, inventory management—as separate problems. Their board viewed each business unit in isolation, while their C-suite optimized individual functions. Meanwhile, Walmart understood retail as an integrated system where online, physical stores, and supply chains formed an interconnected whole.

Traditional Retail Thinking at Sears:

Board Level:
- Evaluated each business unit separately
- Tracked store-by-store performance
- Measured online sales in isolation
- Viewed inventory as a store-level issue
- Assessed digital transformation through IT metrics
- Treated e-commerce as a separate business

C-Suite Level:
- Managed stores independently
- Ran online operations separately
- Maintained separate inventory systems
- Created competing internal structures
- Optimized individual functions
- Measured departmental efficiency

Walmart's Systems Approach:

Board Level:
- Understood retail as an integrated ecosystem
- Recognized how online and physical stores complement each other
- Viewed supply chain as a competitive advantage
- Measured success through total customer experience
- Built technology as a system enabler
- Fostered cross-channel innovation

C-Suite Level:

- Created integrated omnichannel operations
- Developed unified inventory systems
- Built seamless customer experiences
- Implemented cross-functional teams
- Maintained flexible fulfillment options
- Measured total system performance

Today, Walmart thrives while Sears—once America's largest retailer with 3,500 stores and 1% of the entire U.S. GDP—exists only as a cautionary tale of collapse. In just 50 years, Sears fell from commanding $8.9 billion in annual sales to bankruptcy, not because they lacked resources, technology, or market position, but because they failed to understand how retail works as a system to enable resilience against the disruption brought about by competition such as Walmart. A 132-year legacy of success crumbled because they couldn't shift from linear to systems thinking.

Consider Netflix's transformation from DVD rental to global streaming leader. At its peak in 2004, Blockbuster commanded 9,000 stores globally with $5.9 billion in revenue, employing over 84,000 people. Traditional competitors like Blockbuster viewed their business as a series of independent operations—stores, inventory, customer service. Netflix understood entertainment as a complex system where content, delivery, technology, and customer behavior all interconnected.

Blockbuster's Linear Thinking:

Board Level:
- Focused on store profitability metrics
- Tracked rental volumes by location
- Measured success through late fees
- Viewed online as a separate channel
- Assessed competition by physical presence
- Treated customer data as transaction records

C-Suite Level:

SYSTEMS THINKING AND RESILIENCE

- Managed stores as independent units
- Optimized inventory location by location
- Built systems around physical rentals
- Maintained separate online operations
- Responded to local market changes
- Measured success through store metrics

Netflix's Systems Approach:

Board Level:
- Understood entertainment as an ecosystem
- Recognized how viewing habits shape content needs
- Saw technology as an enabler of customer experience
- Measured success through engagement patterns
- Built content strategy around viewing data
- Fostered innovation across the platform

C-Suite Level:
- Created integrated recommendation systems
- Developed predictive content algorithms
- Built technology that shaped viewing habits
- Implemented rapid feedback loops
- Maintained flexible content delivery
- Measured whole-system performance

The results proved transformative. In just six years, from 2004 to 2010, Blockbuster went from market dominance to bankruptcy, while Netflix's systems thinking enabled them to not only survive but build resilience against future disruptions. When streaming technology emerged, Netflix had already developed the systemic thinking needed to transform their entire organization. Today, this same systems approach enables Netflix to maintain resilience against new disruptors like Disney+ and Amazon Prime. Meanwhile, Blockbuster, trapped in linear thinking, became another casualty of failing to build true organizational resilience.

This pattern extends beyond entertainment. Consider how Apple transformed their supply chain under Tim Cook. Before Cook, Apple approached supply chain like most technology companies—as a linear sequence of steps from manufacturing to delivery. Cook understood it as an intricate system where production, inventory, transportation, and market demand all influenced each other.

Traditional Tech Supply Chain Thinking:

Board Level:
- Tracked production quotas
- Monitored inventory levels
- Measured shipping times
- Viewed suppliers as independent contractors
- Assessed costs component by component
- Treated manufacturing as separate from innovation

C-Suite Level:
- Managed factories independently
- Optimized individual transportation routes
- Built buffer inventories at each stage
- Maintained separate regional operations
- Responded to problems sequentially
- Measured efficiency by department

Apple's Systems Approach:

Board Level:
- Understood supply chain as competitive advantage
- Recognized how production capability enables innovation
- Saw inventory as part of customer experience
- Measured success through system flexibility
- Built long-term supplier relationships
- Fostered innovation in manufacturing

SYSTEMS THINKING AND RESILIENCE

C-Suite Level:
- Created integrated production networks
- Developed dynamic inventory management
- Built real-time feedback systems
- Implemented rapid response capabilities
- Maintained manufacturing flexibility
- Measured total system performance

The results transformed Apple's business. While competitors struggled with product launches and supply disruptions, Apple could launch new products globally and adapt quickly to market changes. This wasn't just about efficiency—it was about building resilience through systems thinking.

When COVID-19 disrupted global supply chains in 2020, the stark difference between linear and systems thinking became clear in the athletic apparel industry. Nike and Under Armour, both facing identical external challenges, experienced dramatically different outcomes based on how they understood their supply networks. Under Armour, with 2019 revenues of $5.3 billion, saw sales plummet 23% in 2020. Nike, having built resilience through systems thinking, not only weathered the disruption but saw digital sales surge 82%, with total revenue recovering to pre-pandemic levels within a year.

Consider the contrast between their approaches. Under Armour approached each supply challenge separately:

Board Level:
- Tracked factory closures individually
- Monitored regional inventory gaps
- Measured shipping delays in isolation
- Viewed each supplier independently
- Assessed problems market by market
- Treated online and retail as separate channels

C-Suite Level:
- Managed crisis responses sequentially

- Solved transportation issues one by one
- Built inventory buffers everywhere
- Created separate regional solutions
- Responded to each bottleneck individually
- Measured recovery through individual metrics

Nike's systems approach proved far more resilient:

Board Level:
- Understood their supply network as an ecosystem
- Recognized how disruptions cascade through the system
- Saw digital capability as key to adaptation
- Measured resilience through system flexibility
- Built supplier networks, not just relationships
- Fostered innovation in distribution methods

C-Suite Level:
- Created dynamic production shifting
- Developed integrated inventory management
- Built digital consumer connections
- Implemented rapid market feedback
- Maintained flexible fulfillment options
- Measured total system performance

The results went beyond just surviving the pandemic. By the end of 2021, Nike had increased their direct-to-consumer sales by 40%, captured an additional 12% of market share from competitors, and demonstrated how systems thinking creates lasting resilience. Under Armour, still struggling to recover two years later, saw their market capitalization drop by 50% as their linear thinking left them unable to adapt to the new retail reality. This wasn't about better crisis management—it was about understanding how their organization functioned as a system and building the resilience to thrive through disruption.

Building True Resilience

SYSTEMS THINKING AND RESILIENCE

This fundamental difference in thinking—linear versus systemic—determines whether organizations can build true resilience. Consider how Amazon approaches their business. They don't see themselves as just a retailer, a cloud provider, or a logistics company. They understand their organization as a complex system where each element strengthens the others.

Traditional companies often fail to build resilience because they:

Board Level:
- Create crisis plans for individual scenarios
- Monitor risks in isolation
- View capabilities as separate assets
- Treat innovation as a department function
- Measure resilience through individual metrics
- Focus on protecting existing operations

C-Suite Level:
- Build redundancy without flexibility
- Manage crises sequentially
- Optimize individual functions
- Maintain separate backup systems
- Respond to problems in isolation
- Measure recovery through single metrics

Amazon's systemic approach to resilience:

Board Level:
- Understands resilience as organizational capability
- Recognizes how different businesses reinforce each other
- Sees innovation as a system property
- Measures adaptability across the organization
- Builds capabilities that strengthen the whole system
- Fosters experimentation at every level

C-Suite Level:

- Creates integrated adaptive capabilities
- Develops cross-functional solutions
- Builds rapid learning systems
- Implements continuous feedback
- Maintains flexible operations
- Measures system-wide adaptation

The difference becomes clear in how these approaches affect Ends, Ways, and Means...

Ends, Ways, and Means Through a Systems Lens

Understanding how systems thinking changes our Ends, Ways, and Means framework is crucial for building true resilience. Consider how Microsoft transformed under Satya Nadella. In 2014, Microsoft's traditional linear thinking had left them missing cloud computing, mobile technology, and facing irrelevance in a changing tech landscape. Their market value of $300 billion reflected an organization trapped in outdated ways of thinking. Contrast this with today's Microsoft, valued at over $3 trillion, leading in cloud, AI, and enterprise technology—not because they simply adopted new technologies, but because they fundamentally changed how they thought about their organization as a system.

Traditional Ends, Ways, and Means thinking:

Board Level Ends:
- Windows market share targets
- Office suite revenue goals
- Enterprise license metrics
- Product launch timelines
- Competitor displacement goals
- Cost reduction targets

C-Suite Level Ways:
- Linear product development
- Sequential market entry

SYSTEMS THINKING AND RESILIENCE

- Department-by-department execution
- Individual project tracking
- Siloed responsibility
- Metric-based management

Resource-Based Means:
- Budget allocations
- Headcount by department
- Technology investments
- Training programs
- Process improvements
- Infrastructure projects

Microsoft's systems approach transformed this framework:

System-Based Ends:
- Building adaptive capability
- Developing ecosystem strength
- Creating sustainable innovation
- Enabling continuous evolution
- Fostering market resilience
- Growing system value

Integrated Ways:
- Cross-functional capabilities
- Continuous adaptation
- Ecosystem development
- Rapid experimentation
- Collaborative innovation
- System-wide learning

Capability-Based Means:
- Innovation networks
- Learning systems
- Adaptive technologies

- Collaborative platforms
- Knowledge networks
- System enablers

The results demonstrate the power of systems thinking in building resilience. While competitors like IBM struggled with digital transformation, shedding revenue and market share, Microsoft's cloud business grew from $0 to $120 billion annually in less than a decade. When AI emerged as a disruptive force, Microsoft's systemic resilience enabled them to rapidly integrate and scale AI capabilities across their entire organization. This wasn't just about better execution—it was about building an organization capable of continuous adaptation through systems thinking.

The Leadership Challenge

Understanding how systems thinking enables resilience demands fundamentally different leadership at both governance and execution levels. Consider how PepsiCo transformed under Indra Nooyi. In 2006, PepsiCo was primarily a beverage and snack company, with 70% of revenue from sugary drinks and processed snacks. Traditional leadership would have optimized these existing lines—instead, Nooyi saw PepsiCo as part of a larger health, wellness, and environmental system. This systems thinking enabled PepsiCo to grow revenue from $35 billion to $63 billion while building resilience against changing consumer preferences and environmental pressures.

Contrast this with Kraft Heinz's linear leadership approach:

Board Level:
- Quarterly profit targets
- Cost-cutting initiatives
- Brand-by-brand metrics
- Individual product performance
- Direct competitor analysis
- Short-term margin goals

SYSTEMS THINKING AND RESILIENCE

C-Suite Level:
- Department efficiency drives
- Immediate cost savings
- Sequential product launches
- Market share targets
- Production optimization
- Linear growth plans

This linear thinking led Kraft Heinz to write down their brand value by $15.4 billion in 2019, while PepsiCo's systems approach created resilience through:

Board Level:
- Understanding food systems holistically
- Recognizing interconnections between health, sustainability, and profit
- Seeing how consumer trends reshape entire categories
- Building long-term environmental resilience
- Fostering innovation across categories
- Measuring success through system adaptation

C-Suite Level:
- Creating integrated product portfolios
- Developing sustainable supply chains
- Building health-focused capabilities
- Implementing environmental initiatives
- Maintaining flexible production systems
- Measuring whole-system performance

The results were transformative. While Kraft Heinz struggled with changing consumer preferences, PepsiCo built resilience by transforming 40% of their portfolio to healthier options, reducing environmental impact by 25%, and maintaining growth during market disruptions. Today, PepsiCo demonstrates how systems thinking creates lasting organizational resilience—not just adapting to change, but anticipating and shaping it.

The Future of Resilient Leadership

The evidence is clear: the organizations that thrive aren't necessarily those with the strongest current market positions or the most resources—they're those that understand and operate as systems. Consider how this plays out across industries we've examined. Boeing, with decades of aviation leadership, saw $20 billion in market value erased and their reputation devastated because they couldn't build systemic resilience. Blockbuster, with 9,000 stores and $5.9 billion in revenue, collapsed in just six years through linear thinking. Sears fell from commanding 1% of U.S. GDP to bankruptcy by failing to understand retail as a system.

Meanwhile, organizations that embrace systems thinking build lasting resilience. Microsoft transformed from a declining software company to a $3 trillion cloud and AI leader. Nike turned supply chain disruption into 82% digital sales growth while competitors faltered. PepsiCo reshaped their entire portfolio while growing revenue from $35 billion to $63 billion.

The choice facing leaders today is stark but clear:

Board Level Must:
- Move beyond traditional oversight metrics
- Understand their organizations as complex systems
- Guide long-term capability development
- Foster innovation across boundaries
- Build resilience into governance
- Measure success through adaptation

C-Suite Level Must:
- Create integrated solutions
- Develop adaptive capabilities
- Build feedback mechanisms
- Enable rapid learning
- Lead systemic change

SYSTEMS THINKING AND RESILIENCE

- Transform organizational thinking

This isn't about merely adapting to disruption—it's about building organizations that gain capability through each challenge they face. The transformation demands that leaders challenge fundamental assumptions about how organizations function and develop comfort with complexity and ambiguity. As we've seen through numerous examples, organizations that fail to make this shift pay an increasingly heavy price. Those that succeed understand a crucial truth: true resilience emerges when organizations operate as integrated systems, not collections of metrics.

8

THE REALITY OF RESILIENCE

Let me show you what really happens when organizations try to build resilience. Forget the success stories we've explored - let's talk about the messy reality of resistance, pushback, and organizational inertia. It's like watching a slow-motion car crash where everyone sees the collision coming but nobody turns the wheel.

Take Kodak in the early 2000s. They weren't just aware of the digital revolution - they'd invented it. They had everything going for them:
- Market dominance and a legendary brand
- World-class R&D capabilities
- A war chest of financial resources
- Crystal-clear visibility of the digital threat ahead

Yet there they sat, like a deer in headlights, unable to make the necessary changes. Why? Because understanding the need for resilience isn't enough. You have to overcome the forces actively working against it - the comfortable inertia of success, the fear of cannibalizing existing products, the organizational antibodies that attack any significant change. Kodak saw the future coming but couldn't get out of its own way.

The Reality of Organizational Resistance

Building resilience is going to get pushback – it often defies short-term goal setting, does not show a traditional return on investment, and it will shake up the status quo, fiefdoms, and sacred cows. For all of these reasons, in addition to the fact that humans are not wired well to accept change, organizations are known to resist improvement efforts, even to their own detriment. Maybe the resistance will come from only certain areas, or it could be across the board, but it is the exception for it not to be somewhere in the mix, not the norm. Let's take another look at what happened at Boeing, by framing it through the lens of resistance . Their technical experts knew about potential issues with the 737 MAX. Their safety teams raised concerns. Their engineers suggested alternative approaches. But resistance emerged at both governance and execution levels:

Board Level Resistance:
- Prioritized shareholder returns over safety
- Maintained traditional oversight models
- Resisted expanding risk governance
- Defaulted to financial metrics

C-Suite Level Resistance:
- Pushed for quarterly earnings
- Accelerated market delivery
- Minimized technical concerns
- Maintained existing processes

Cultural Barriers:

Board Level:
- "We've always governed this way"
- Success-bred governance complacency
- Risk-averse oversight mentality

C-Suite Level:
- "We've always operated this way"
- Operational complacency
- Middle management defensiveness

Structural Obstacles:

Board Level:
- Rigid governance frameworks
- Traditional committee structures
- Misaligned oversight incentives

THE REALITY OF RESILIENCE

C-Suite Level:
- Siloed information flows
- Rigid reporting structures
- Misaligned operational incentives

This multi-level resistance created a perfect storm - governance couldn't direct resilience while operations couldn't build it.

The Success Pattern

As much as Boeing shows the implications of resistance, other organizations show the benefits of tackling it head on. Look at how Microsoft overcame resistance barriers at both levels. Their approach shows how governance and execution must work together to defeat resistance:

Board Level Action:
- Empowered new strategic direction
- Restructured oversight committees
- Changed performance evaluation criteria
- Supported long-term transformation over short-term results

C-Suite Level Action (under Nadella):
- Dismantled entrenched product groups
- Replaced resistant executives
- Flattened rigid hierarchies
- Built change capability

This two-level approach was crucial - board-level support gave Nadella's C-suite the authority and resources to drive real transformation. His approach wasn't just about vision - it was about systematically dismantling resistance points:

1. Financial Restructuring
- Changed bonus structures

- Rebuilt performance metrics
- Realigned incentives
- Created transformation funding

2. Power Structure Reality
Instead of fighting existing power structures, he:
- Gave influential leaders new challenges
- Created opportunities for change advocates
- Removed resistance points
- Built new power bases around adaptation

3. Cultural Rewiring
- Eliminated stack ranking
- Rewarded learning from failure
- Created cross-functional authority
- Built adaptation into promotions

The Cost of Resistance – A Final Example

Perhaps the Boeing example is a bit too much, and you are thinking that their resistance and impact on human life is not comparable to your organization. All right, fair point. Then let's look at what resistance cost General Electric. Under Jeff Immelt, they:
- Knew they needed digital transformation
- Had the resources to change
- Understood the competitive threat
- Saw the market shifting

But they couldn't overcome internal resistance. Result?
- Lost $500 billion in market value
- Dropped from Dow Jones Industrial Average
- Eroded competitive position
- Damaged organizational capability

So you have to ask, if a company resists enacting change to even the basic concepts that are needed to sustain day-today core business operations and targets, how well do you see it willing to embrace the changes needed to build resilience? As you let that sink in, take a good look around you, and ask…where do you honestly see your leadership team on this spectrum?

The Strategy Reality: Addressing Resistance with Decisive Action

When it comes to addressing resistance, there's a clear strategy that works. Resilient leaders don't waste time trying to win over those actively blocking progress—they act decisively to clear the path forward. Both AMD's Lisa Su and JP Morgan Chase's Jamie Dimon provide two great examples of how decisive leadership can overcome entrenched opposition and enable transformation.

Lisa Su's success at AMD highlights how to dismantle resistance effectively:

What she didn't do:
- Launch change programs
- Create transformation offices
- Roll out new values statements
- Reorganize reporting structures

What she did instead:
- Removed resistant leaders quickly
- Created immediate wins to build momentum
- Built new power structures aligned with her vision
- Rewired decision-making processes to ensure adaptability

Su's approach demonstrates a critical truth: resistance to change isn't solved by more programs or persuasion. While she undoubtedly invested in aligning her team, she didn't waste time trying to convince entrenched opponents to change. When faced with individuals who actively hindered progress, she made the hard call—removing them.

This isn't just theoretical. I've seen firsthand how a single resistant VP can derail a global transformation effort, refusing to adapt despite countless "alignment" sessions and appeals to see the bigger picture. Resistance at the leadership level is like a virus—it spreads, undermining morale, momentum, and progress. Su's example serves as a best practice: when resistance becomes a liability, decisive action is the only solution.

Jamie Dimon's leadership at JP Morgan Chase during their AI transformation reinforces this point. Dimon didn't just announce bold new initiatives—he reshaped the organizational power dynamic to ensure success:
- Replacing resistant executives who blocked progress
- Rebuilding incentive structures to reward alignment with transformation goals
- Creating new power centers that championed AI adoption
- Eliminating key blockers who stood in the way

This isn't about being harsh—it's about being clear. Organizations don't resist change; people in power resist change. Leaders like Su and Dimon understand that clearing the way for progress is just as critical as the transformation itself.

Giving people a chance to adapt is fair, but waiting too long for entrenched opponents to change only jeopardizes the entire effort. Leaders like Su and Dimon prove that decisive action isn't about being ruthless—it's about prioritizing progress and ensuring the organization has the right people in place to move forward.

The Three Critical Shifts

Breaking resistance and driving transformation requires more than announcing new strategies—it demands a deliberate restructuring of resources, power, and success metrics. Microsoft's transformation under Satya Nadella demonstrates how these shifts clear the path for progress and resilience:

1. Resource Control

Nadella redirected the flow of organizational resources to prioritize adaptability and innovation:
- Moved budgets to leaders championing transformation.

THE REALITY OF RESILIENCE

- Created new investment streams to fund adaptive initiatives.
- Built independent transformation funding to bypass bureaucratic bottlenecks.
- Bypassed traditional allocations that reinforced the status quo.

By taking control of where resources flowed, Nadella empowered those driving change and removed barriers that protected outdated priorities.

2. Power Redistribution

Power in an organization is a critical lever for change. Nadella reshaped Microsoft's leadership landscape to align with its future:
- Promoted advocates of adaptation into influential roles.
- Sidelined resistance points, removing blockers from positions of authority.
- Created new authority structures that supported transformation efforts.
- Built transformation momentum by ensuring decision-makers shared a unified vision.

These changes sent a clear message: power would no longer reside in preserving the status quo but in advancing the organization's future.

3. Redefining Success

Nadella understood that traditional success metrics often reward stability over progress. To drive resilience, he redefined how success was measured and rewarded:
- Changed performance metrics to emphasize adaptability and long-term capability.
- Rebuilt bonus structures to incentivize transformation efforts.
- Created new career paths aligned with the organization's future needs.
- Rewarded adaptation capability as a core leadership trait.

By aligning success with resilience, Nadella ensured that transformation wasn't just an initiative—it became part of Microsoft's DNA.

The Human Reality

Let's be clear about what happens on the ground: when organizations embark on transformation, the greatest challenges often stem not from technology or strategy, but from people—human beings protecting their roles, authority, and metrics. PepsiCo's digital transformation is a case study in navigating this reality. As they moved forward, they faced the same entrenched resistance that plagues most organizations:

Mid-Level Reality
- Managers protecting their teams and established workflows
- Directors defending their budgets and existing priorities
- VPs maintaining their authority and influence
- Everyone protecting their metrics, fearing the unknown consequences of change

Instead of confronting this resistance head-on, PepsiCo chose a more strategic approach. Under the leadership of Athina Kanioura, Chief Strategy and Transformation Officer, they implemented tactics that both mitigated resistance and unlocked new opportunities:

- Created new opportunities for adaptable leaders: By emphasizing upskilling across all levels of the organization, they empowered individuals to thrive in new roles aligned with the transformation.
- Built parallel power structures: PepsiCo developed alternative systems and teams that drove innovation without dismantling the existing hierarchy too quickly.
- Developed alternative career paths: Employees were offered clear pathways to advance their careers by contributing to the transformation, which reduced fear and resistance.

THE REALITY OF RESILIENCE

- Established transformation credentials: By formalizing transformation skills as part of career development, they incentivized leaders to adapt and align with the company's new direction.

Kanioura emphasized that the transformation wasn't about job elimination but about reshaping the company's culture and business through technology. By framing the change as an opportunity rather than a threat, PepsiCo minimized friction and created a workforce that embraced the future.

Transformation requires addressing the human side of change as much as the operational or technological. Organizations that succeed—like PepsiCo—don't waste energy battling resistance directly. Instead, they redirect it, creating pathways for individuals to adapt, grow, and thrive within the new vision.

The Career Dynamic

Career progression is at the heart of resistance during transformation—people want to see a path forward for themselves. Microsoft's transformation under Satya Nadella addressed this directly by reshaping how careers were defined and advanced:

Old Path They Eliminated:
- Time in role: Promotions based on tenure rather than impact
- Budget managed: Rewarding leaders for the size of their financial control rather than their adaptability
- Team size: Valuing the number of direct reports over the ability to lead effectively
- Project completion: Focusing on ticking off tasks rather than driving meaningful change

New Path They Created:
- Adaptation capability: Leaders were evaluated on their ability to pivot and thrive amid disruption.
- Innovation implementation: Those who successfully introduced new ideas and systems were rewarded.

- Cross-functional impact: Individuals who could bridge silos and drive collaboration saw their careers flourish.
- Transformation success: Promotion was tied to the measurable contributions to the company's transformation.

By aligning career progression with transformation goals, Microsoft ensured that leaders were incentivized to embrace and champion change rather than resist it. This approach also reassured employees that adapting to the new vision was not just necessary, but an opportunity for growth and advancement.

The Personal Stakes

Transformation isn't just about shifting strategies or processes—it directly impacts individuals' sense of security and identity within an organization. Where most companies fail is in ignoring this deeply personal dimension of change. NVIDIA's approach offers a blueprint for addressing these stakes effectively:

They acknowledged:
- Career uncertainties: Employees feared whether their roles would survive the transformation.
- Skill obsolescence fears: Rapid advancements in technology raised concerns about their ability to keep up.
- Authority disruption: Long-standing leaders worried about losing their influence or relevance.
- Status challenges: Shifts in organizational priorities created unease about perceived importance and recognition.

Then they built:
- Clear transition paths: Employees were shown exactly how they could move from their current roles to future opportunities.
- Skill development programs: NVIDIA invested in upskilling at all levels, enabling employees to remain valuable contributors.
- New authority structures: Leaders who embraced transformation were given new roles that reinforced their value to the organization.

THE REALITY OF RESILIENCE

- Future leadership roles: High-potential employees were developed and positioned for roles within the reimagined organization.

NVIDIA's acknowledgment of the human side of change wasn't just empathetic—it was strategic. By addressing personal stakes head-on, they minimized resistance, retained key talent, and ensured that employees saw the transformation as an opportunity rather than a threat.

Sustaining Momentum: Overcoming Resistance

Transformations succeed when organizations build momentum so strong that resistance becomes irrelevant. Across organizations like Amazon, Adobe, Microsoft, and ServiceNow, a few key practices emerge as essential for maintaining progress and overcoming opposition at every level.

1. Reshaping Governance for Long-Term Impact

Amazon's transformation highlights the critical role of governance in building and sustaining momentum. At the board level, they shifted their focus away from short-term priorities and embraced resilience-based oversight:

- Old Oversight They Killed: Quarterly performance focus, traditional risk metrics, and short-term value measures.
- New Direction They Set: Long-term capability building, innovation investment mandates, and resilience-based evaluation.
- By aligning the board's focus with transformation goals, Amazon ensured the resources and authority to drive sustained change.

2. Driving C-Suite Execution for Transformation Success

Momentum must also be sustained at the operational level, as Amazon's and Microsoft's approaches demonstrate. Leaders at the top rejected outdated operational metrics and prioritized building the capabilities needed for continuous transformation:

- Old Operations They Killed: Individual performance metrics, department efficiency targets, cost management, and resource utilization standards.
- New Capabilities They Built: Innovation implementation, cross-functional collaboration, continuous adaptation, and rapid experimentation.

By focusing on agility and adaptability, these organizations ensured their operations evolved alongside their strategic goals, making resistance futile.

3. Accelerating Change Through Speed and Results

ServiceNow's transformation demonstrates a key truth: speed defeats resistance. Rather than waiting for consensus or perfect plans, they prioritized rapid wins and visible impact:

- What They Avoided: Consensus building, gradual implementation, universal buy-in, and perfect planning.
- What They Did Instead: Quick capability builds, rapid success creation, fast power shifts, and immediate impact demonstration.

When transformation efforts show clear results quickly, opposition loses credibility, and momentum becomes unstoppable.

4. Using Success to Silence Opposition

Adobe's shift from packaged software to cloud services exemplifies how early wins can make resistance irrelevant. They didn't force compliance or mandate change; instead, they focused on delivering undeniable results:

- What They Created: Clear early wins, visible momentum, undeniable results, and success stories that made resistance look obsolete.

THE REALITY OF RESILIENCE

- What They Achieved: Revenue growth, market expansion, capability development, and a competitive edge that spoke louder than any opposition.

When employees and leaders see the tangible benefits of transformation, resistance naturally fades.

5. *Establishing New Power Centers*

Microsoft's success highlights the importance of creating new structures and leaders aligned with transformation goals. Instead of relying on existing hierarchies, they:

- Built new capability centers
- Created transformation hubs
- Developed leaders focused on adaptation
- Established resilience as a core organizational structure

By redistributing power and authority to those driving transformation, Microsoft ensured that resistance had no place to take root.

The Reality Check

Organizations that sustain transformation don't waste time trying to convert everyone. Microsoft, Amazon, and Adobe all accepted that:

- Some leaders wouldn't change
- Some managers would leave
- Some teams would resist
- Some processes would need to die

Instead, they focused on building new capabilities, creating clear successes, and developing momentum so strong that resistance became irrelevant.

The Lesson

Transformation isn't about perfection or universal agreement—it's about creating a future so compelling that those who can't adapt are left behind. Success breeds momentum, momentum overcomes resistance, and resilience ensures the change lasts.

The Governance Shield

Let me show you the dirty secret of organizational resistance. Most people think resistance comes from middle management or front-line employees. But here's the truth: The strongest resistance hides behind governance structures. It's not just people resisting change - it's governance systems protecting them.

Look at what really happened at Boeing. Everyone focuses on the operational resistance to safety concerns. But the real story is how their governance structure shielded that resistance:

- Risk committees that prioritized production schedules
- Audit processes that emphasized compliance over safety
- Oversight frameworks that rewarded speed over quality
- Board committees that protected existing practices

This governance shield made operational resistance virtually bulletproof. Safety concerns couldn't penetrate governance protection. Technical warnings couldn't overcome structural barriers. The result? Tragedy, because governance structures amplified resistance instead of enabling resilience.

Compare that to how Microsoft dismantled their governance shield. When Nadella started transformation, he didn't just fight operational resistance. He worked with the board to rebuild governance structures:

Old Shields They Demolished:
- Performance committees that blocked innovation
- Risk frameworks that prevented experimentation
- Oversight processes that maintained status quo

THE REALITY OF RESILIENCE

- Governance systems that reinforced silos

New Structures They Built:
- Innovation-focused governance
- Experimentation-enabling frameworks
- Adaptation-driving processes
- Collaboration-supporting systems

This governance evolution stripped resistance of its structural protection. When people tried to block change, they found no governance shield to hide behind.

The pattern is clear across industries. Failed transformations didn't just face operational resistance - they crashed into governance shields:

- Intel's governance protected chip manufacturing dominance until TSMC won
- IBM's governance shielded software licensing until cloud computing won
- Kodak's governance defended film processing until digital imaging won

The winners didn't just overcome resistance - they dismantled its protective structures. Look at how AMD rebuilt governance under Lisa Su:

- They didn't just change metrics - they rebuilt measurement systems
- They didn't just set new goals - they recreated goal-setting processes
- They didn't just demand innovation; they restructured innovation governance

This matters because resistance isn't just about people - it's about the structures protecting them. You can't build resilience by fighting resistance directly. You have to dismantle its governance shield first.

The message is clear: Before you tackle operational resistance, rebuild governance structures. Traditional governance protects traditional thinking. Only resilient governance can enable true transformation.

The Final Reality

Successful organizations don't just manage resistance—they make it irrelevant. These aren't comfortable lessons, but they are the truths that define resilience in a world of constant disruption.

The Truth About Change

NVIDIA's AI transformation highlights the reality of change: not everyone will adapt, and not every role will survive.

They accepted:
- Not everyone would make it
- Some careers would end
- Certain roles would disappear
- Power structures would shift

But they also:
- Created new opportunities
- Built clear transition paths
- Developed future roles
- Established new power centers

Their ability to confront these truths while creating a future for those who could evolve demonstrates why they continue to lead in a competitive, disrupted market.

The Market Truth

Amazon's approach to transformation reveals an unyielding reality: the market doesn't wait for internal struggles to resolve.

They understood:

THE REALITY OF RESILIENCE

- Markets don't care about internal resistance
- Competitors don't wait for consensus
- Customers don't consider your comfort
- Innovation doesn't respect hierarchy

Their response:
- Built capability regardless of resistance
- Created success despite opposition
- Developed momentum past obstacles
- Made adaptation inevitable

Amazon's relentless focus on delivering results, regardless of internal resistance, shows why they continue to dominate and redefine industries.

The Leadership Truth

Microsoft's transformation under Satya Nadella uncovers the hardest lesson of all: resilient leadership requires making the tough calls. Leaders must:
- Make difficult decisions about people and roles
- Shift power structures to align with transformation goals
- Create new hierarchies that support the future vision
- Build entirely new futures for their organizations

This isn't about ruthlessness—it's about clarity. Resilient leaders act not out of harshness but necessity, because:
- Markets demand adaptation
- Competition thrives on change
- Success is impossible without capability
- Survival depends on resilience

Nadella's leadership demonstrates that success isn't about easing into transformation—it's about leading it decisively and unapologetically.

The Closing Truth

The survivors in every industry aren't those who manage resistance best—they're the ones who make resistance irrelevant through undeniable success.

In a world of constant disruption, the cost of building resilience is high, but the cost of failing to build it is far higher. Organizations either adapt, evolve, and thrive, or they become cautionary tales of missed opportunity.

The choice is simple: Build resilience—or become a case study in failure. There is no middle ground.

9

RESILIENCE FOR SMALLER ORGANIZATIONS

Let me tell you about two companies that faced AI disruption in 2023. One was IBM, with 350,000 employees and billions in resources. The other was Jasper AI, with just 80 employees and limited capital. When ChatGPT launched, IBM spent months navigating internal committees, governance structures, and enterprise deployment plans. Jasper completely pivoted their product strategy in weeks, retrained their entire team, and launched new AI capabilities before IBM's committees had finished their initial assessments.

This isn't a story about David beating Goliath. It's about how organizational size affects resilience in fundamentally different ways. Yes, IBM has vastly more resources. Yes, they have deeper expertise and broader reach. But Jasper had something more valuable in a moment of disruption - they could change course without fighting organizational gravity.

The Scale Reality

Look, I get it: If you're leading a 200-person company or serving on the board of a 50-person startup, much of what's written about organizational resilience probably feels out of touch with your day-to-day reality. You don't have:

- Multiple board committees
- Layers of management
- Large transformation budgets
- Dedicated innovation teams

Most resilience literature assumes you have resources and structures that simply don't exist in smaller organizations. But here's what's fascinating - this apparent disadvantage often becomes your greatest strength in building true resilience.

Look at what happened when COVID-19 hit the restaurant technology sector. While Toast, a restaurant technology company with 300 employees, transformed their entire business model in weeks, industry giant Oracle took months just to modify their existing products. The difference wasn't resources - it was organizational complexity. Toast didn't have to navigate layers of approval or align multiple divisions. They could see the problem, design a solution, and execute immediately.

The Three Core Advantages of Small Organizations

Smaller organizations have unique opportunities to turn their size into a genuine resilience advantage. This isn't just about being nimble—it's about capitalizing on structural strengths that larger organizations simply can't replicate, no matter how much they spend or how hard they try.

Decision Velocity

This isn't just about making faster decisions - it's about the compound effect of rapid, iterative decision-making. Look at how Notion, a team collaboration platform, leveraged this advantage:

Large Company Reality:
- 6 weeks to align stakeholders
- 3 months to approve changes
- 6 months to implement
- 1 year to adjust course

Notion's Approach:
- Monday morning: Identified market shift
- Monday afternoon: Aligned entire leadership
- Tuesday: Communicated changes company-wide
- Wednesday: Started implementation

RESILIENCE FOR SMALLER ORGANIZATIONS

- Friday: Already gathering feedback and adjusting

Customer Signal Clarity

Smaller organizations don't just have closer customer relationships - they have clearer customer signals. When Loom noticed shifts in how customers used their video messaging platform, they had:
- Engineers talking directly to users
- Customer support sharing insights instantly
- Product teams testing solutions immediately
- Leadership making decisions based on direct customer feedback

Compare that to large enterprises where customer feedback navigates through:
- Multiple reporting layers
- Various department filters
- Numerous approval stages
- Multiple interpretation cycles

Cultural Adaptation Speed

This might be the most powerful advantage. Look at how Vercel, a web development platform, transformed their entire approach to deployment:

Large Enterprise Timeline:
- 6 months to communicate change
- 1 year to shift mindsets
- 18 months to see behavior change
- 2 years to cement new culture

Vercel's Reality:
- Week 1: New direction set
- Week 2: Team processes changed
- Week 3: New behaviors visible
- Week 4: Culture shift taking hold

These three core advantages - Decision Velocity, Customer Signal Clarity, and Cultural Adaptation Speed - aren't just nice-to-have features of smaller organizations. They're powerful structural advantages that form the foundation of true resilience. When Figma competed against Adobe, or when Notion went up against Microsoft, they weren't succeeding despite their size - they were winning because of it. The key is understanding how to leverage these advantages systematically rather than treating them as occasional benefits. In the sections ahead, we'll explore exactly how to turn these structural advantages into practical resilience that can withstand any disruption.

Translating Big Company Lessons

Here's where smaller organizations often go wrong - they try to copy big company resilience programs. That's exactly backward. The principles scale down, but the implementation needs to be radically different.

Look at how Copper CRM, with 250 employees, applied the Ends, Ways, and Means framework:

Ends: They didn't write a 50-page strategic plan. Their leadership team spent one day defining what had to be true for them to matter in three years.

Ways: Instead of creating transformation offices and change programs, they:
- Identified three critical capabilities they needed to build
- Assigned clear owners for each
- Created weekly check-ins to maintain momentum

Means: Rather than huge budgets, they focused on:
- Reallocating existing resources
- Building internal expertise
- Creating learning opportunities in daily work

The result? They transformed from a basic CRM to an AI-enhanced platform faster than Salesforce could roll out their first AI feature.

The Implementation Playbook

Let me be clear about something - your size means you can't afford the luxury of slow transformation. When Calendly, then a 100-person company, saw the shift to remote work creating new scheduling challenges, they didn't launch a transformation program. Instead, they created what I call a "Minimal Viable Resilience" approach.

Here's what they did instead of traditional big-company transformation:

Speed Over Scale
- Monday: Leadership team evaluates market shift
- Tuesday: New priorities communicated to entire company
- Wednesday: Teams begin rebuilding capabilities
- Thursday: First changes hit production
- Friday: Customer feedback starts flowing

Compare that to how a large enterprise would handle it:
- Month 1: Evaluate market conditions
- Month 2-3: Plan transformation initiative
- Month 4-6: Begin pilot programs
- Month 7-9: Initial rollout
- Month 10-12: Full deployment

The small organization advantage isn't just about speed - it's about learning velocity. When Figma, with just 150 employees, started competing with Adobe's massive design tools empire, they turned their size into an advantage:

Learning Loops They Built:
- Designers talking directly to users daily
- Engineers deploying changes hourly

- Product teams adjusting features weekly
- Entire company pivoting monthly

Resource-Efficient Capability Building

Here's where smaller organizations can actually outmaneuver larger ones. Look at how Vercel, a 200-person company, built new capabilities without massive budgets:

Instead of Traditional Approaches:
- Hiring expensive consultants
- Creating dedicated transformation teams
- Running large training programs
- Building separate innovation units

They Did This:
- Paired every team member with someone learning a new skill
- Created "capability hours" where work stopped for learning
- Built learning directly into project execution
- Made skill-sharing part of every team meeting

Common Pitfalls and Solutions

Small organizations often stumble into the same traps when trying to build resilience, mistakenly adopting strategies designed for companies ten times their size. These missteps don't just slow progress—they can derail transformation entirely. But here's the good news: the smartest small organizations avoid these traps by leveraging their unique strengths, crafting solutions that are tailored to their size, agility, and focus. Let's break down the two most common pitfalls, and look at how to turn these challenges into opportunities.

Pitfall 1: The Process Trap

Trying to implement big-company processes in a small organization is like putting a truck engine in a motorcycle. Look at how Linear, a 40-person software company, avoided this:

RESILIENCE FOR SMALLER ORGANIZATIONS

Instead of:
- Creating complex approval processes
- Building multiple review layers
- Implementing rigid controls

They Built:
- Simple decision frameworks
- Clear accountability paths
- Rapid feedback loops

Pitfall 2: The Resource Stretch

For small organizations, dedicating entire teams to transformation is often unrealistic. Spreading resources too thin can lead to burnout, stalled progress, and half-hearted implementation. Retool, a 120-person software company, tackled this challenge head-on with a pragmatic and innovative approach:

What they didn't do:
- Create separate transformation teams
- Delay daily operations to prioritize change
- Overload individuals with conflicting responsibilities
- Treat transformation as an "add-on" project; something to get to, but not the core mission

What they did instead:
- Integrated transformation into everyone's job: Ensured that each employee had a role in driving change.
- Built new capabilities through actual work: Focused on learning by doing, embedding transformation tasks into daily workflows.
- Created learning opportunities in operations: Used routine tasks as opportunities to train employees on new systems and skills.
- Rotated staff through critical initiatives: Provided exposure to strategic projects, ensuring cross-functional growth and alignment.

By weaving transformation into the fabric of their operations, Retool avoided the resource stretch and made progress a shared responsibility rather than a siloed burden.

The Path Forward

Let me be clear about what this means for your organization. You don't need massive resources or complex programs to build resilience. What you need is:

1. Clarity of Direction
- One page of strategic intent
- Three critical capabilities to build
- Clear weekly priorities
- Visible progress markers

2. Speed of Learning
- Daily customer feedback
- Weekly capability building
- Monthly strategy adjustments
- Quarterly transformation assessment

3. Focus of Resources
- Every project builds new capabilities
- Every team member learns new skills
- Every customer interaction creates insight
- Every failure generates learning

Look at how Zapier, starting with just 30 people, built a company that now automates work for millions while competing against tech giants. They didn't try to copy enterprise transformation programs. Instead, they:
- Made learning part of daily work
- Built capabilities through real projects
- Created simple but effective feedback loops
- Maintained cultural cohesion through growth

RESILIENCE FOR SMALLER ORGANIZATIONS

The reality is this: Your size isn't a disadvantage in building resilience - it's an advantage if you use it correctly. You can't copy Microsoft's transformation playbook, but you can move faster, learn quicker, and adapt more effectively than they ever could.

The organizations that thrive won't be the ones with the biggest transformation budgets - they'll be the ones that turn their size into an advantage by building resilience into their daily operations.

In the end, resilience isn't about size - it's about building the capability to adapt, learn, and transform before you need to. And in that race, smaller organizations often have the edge.

The only question is: Will you use it?

10

CONCLUSION

I hope by now, the evidence is clear: organizations that succeeded through recent disruptions didn't just have better plans or stronger balance sheets. They did not apply brute force and create sustainability deception. What they had done was build the capability to adapt, learn, and transform before they needed to. They had built true resilience.

As we saw, Microsoft's transformation under Nadella demonstrates what this looks like in practice. In 2014, Microsoft was trapped in linear thinking, missing cloud computing, mobile technology, and facing irrelevance. Their response wasn't to push harder within existing frameworks—a common but fatal mistake. Instead, they fundamentally changed how they understood their organization as a system. The result wasn't just adoption of new technologies, but a complete transformation in how the organization functioned, thought, and adapted.

The contrast with Intel during the same period reveals how linear thinking undermines resilience. Intel had everything traditional metrics suggested they needed: strong financials, market leadership, deep technical expertise. What they lacked was the organizational capability to adapt quickly to market shifts. Their response to challenges—pushing existing processes harder, demanding more from teams, competing primarily on technical specifications—exemplified the dangerous belief that intensity can replace true resilience. The result? They lost manufacturing leadership to TSMC, chip design leadership to AMD, and missed multiple technology cycles.

This pattern repeats across industries. Linear thinking manifests in many destructive ways, but perhaps none so deceptive as the belief that brute force effort can replace true resilience. Consider Circuit City's collapse from $12 billion in revenue to bankruptcy. Their linear response to competition—cutting experienced staff, pushing remaining workers harder, competing solely on price—appeared logical in isolation. But these moves, typical of linear thinking, destroyed the very capabilities needed for adaptation and survival.

Amazon's success reveals the alternative. Their achievement isn't just about e-commerce dominance or technological innovation. It's about understanding that sustainable performance emerges from system capabilities, not unsustainable effort. While traditional retailers tried to compete through price cuts, worker overtime, and cost reduction, Amazon built integrated systems that could adapt and evolve. Their board understood resilience as an organizational capability, while their C-suite built the integrated systems to deliver it.

The financial services sector shows similar patterns. JP Morgan Chase's initial resistance to AI tools, followed by their rapid pivot and $12 billion technology investment, demonstrates how even well-resourced organizations must build the capability to change course quickly. Their experience, like Microsoft's and Amazon's, shows that resilience isn't about having perfect plans—it's about having the organizational capability to adapt when those plans meet reality.

In the automotive industry, Toyota's response to disruption consistently demonstrates this truth about resilience. When the 2008-2009 crisis hit, they didn't just slash costs or demand more from workers—they activated integrated systems built through decades of systems thinking. While GM required government bailout despite intense effort to cut costs and push efficiency, Toyota adapted their production, maintained their workforce capability, and emerged stronger. Today, as the industry faces electric vehicle disruption, this same systemic resilience enables Toyota to evolve while traditional manufacturers struggle despite heroic efforts.

The retail transformation tells an equally compelling story. Walmart's success against Amazon isn't about matching their technology investments or pushing their organization harder—it's about understanding retail as a system where online, physical stores, and supply chains form an interconnected whole. Meanwhile, Sears—once commanding 1% of the entire U.S. GDP—collapsed into bankruptcy not from lack of effort or resources, but from failing to understand how retail works as a system. A 132-year legacy of success crumbled because they couldn't shift from linear to systems thinking.

CONCLUSION

This fundamental distinction between linear and systems thinking reshapes how we understand the Ends, Ways, and Means framework. Organizations trapped in linear thinking reduce Ends to metric targets, view Ways as sequential steps, and treat Means as mere resources to deploy. Those that build true resilience understand that Ends involve building adaptive capability, Ways require integrated approaches, and Means focus on developing system-wide capabilities.

The implications reach beyond individual companies to entire industries. Tesla didn't disrupt the automotive market just through electric vehicles—they did it by building an organization that could adapt and innovate faster than traditional manufacturers. Netflix didn't just beat Blockbuster through better technology—they built an entertainment ecosystem while Blockbuster optimized store operations. In each case, the determining factor wasn't resources, market position, or even leadership vision. It was the organizational capability to adapt, learn, and transform.

The leaders who understand this don't just survive disruption—they use it as fuel for growth. They recognize that today's capabilities, no matter how strong, are just a foundation for building tomorrow's. They know that resilience isn't about having bulletproof systems or perfect plans—it's about building organizations that get stronger through change.

The patterns are clear. The evidence is compelling. Success requires both levels of leadership working in concert. Boards must move beyond traditional oversight to direct true resilience strategy. C-suites must transform from operational execution to capability building. Organizations that thrive aren't just well-managed at either level—they're fundamentally resilient at both. This isn't about governance or execution alone. It's about boards and C-suites together building organizations that shape the future rather than just react to it.

The difference between success and failure in the years ahead won't be determined by current market position, financial strength, or even technological capability. It will be determined by organizational resilience—the ability to adapt, learn, and transform in response to whatever challenges and opportunities emerge.

The future belongs to the resilient.

REFERENCES

Accenture (2021). The race for operational resilience. https://www.accenture.com/us-en/insights/consulting/coronavirus-supply-chain-disruption.

Alexander, J. (2021). Netflix's latest pivot: Gaming. The Verge. https://www.theverge.com/2021/7/20/22585959/netflix-gaming-expansion-video-streaming.

Allison, M. (2019). The North Star: Starbucks' approach to a purpose-driven strategy. Retrieved from https://stories.starbucks.com/stories/2019/the-north-star-starbucks-approach-to-a-purpose-driven-strategy/.

Altman, S. (2023, November 22). The path forward. OpenAI Blog. https://openai.com/blog/the-path-forward.

AMD. (2023, October 31). AMD Reports Third Quarter 2023 Financial Results. AMD Investor Relations.

AMD. (2023). 2022 Annual Report. Advanced Micro Devices, Inc.

Anders, G. (2012, April 4). Inside Amazon's idea machine: How Bezos decodes customers. Forbes. https://www.forbes.com/sites/georgeanders/2012/04/04/inside-amazon-idea-machine-bezos-customers/.

Arbel, T. (2023, April 14). JPMorgan's trading revenue surges as bank navigates crisis. Associated Press.

Argyris, C. (1991). Teaching smart people how to learn. Harvard Business Review, 69(3), 99-109.

Bastian, E. (2020, March 18). A message from Ed Bastian: Delta's response to COVID-19. Delta News Hub.

Bastian, E. (2023). Delta Air Lines: Building resilience through crisis. Harvard Business Review, 101(4), 35-41.

Benioff, M. (2023, December 12). Salesforce announces Einstein Copilot. Salesforce News.

Benioff, M. & Adler, C. (2009). Behind the cloud: The untold story of how Salesforce.com went from idea to billion-dollar company--and revolutionized an industry. John Wiley & Sons.

Bloomberg. (2023, December 15). Microsoft market value tops $3 trillion as AI boom drives gains. Bloomberg News.

Boeing Commercial Airplanes. (2023). Commercial Market Outlook 2023-2042. Boeing Company.

Boeing. (2019). 737 MAX Updates. The Boeing Company Newsroom.

Bort, J. (2023, January 18). Microsoft announces 10,000 job cuts, nearly 5% of its workforce. CNBC.

Christensen, C. M. (1997). The innovator's dilemma: When new technologies cause great firms to fail. Harvard Business School Press.

Collins, J. C. & Porras, J. I. (1994). Built to last: Successful habits of visionary companies. HarperBusiness.

CVS Health. (2023). 2022 Annual Report. CVS Health Corporation.

CVS Health. (2023). The path to healthcare transformation. CVS Health Insights Report.

REFERENCES

Davenport, T. H. & Westerman, G. (2018). Why so many high-profile digital transformations fail. Harvard Business Review, 96(2), 78-85.

Deloitte (2022). The perseverance of resilient leadership: Sustaining impact on the road to Thrive. 2021 Deloitte Global Resilience Report.

Dimon, J. (2023, April). Jamie Dimon on navigating crisis and building organizational resilience. *JPMorgan Chase Shareholder Letter.*

Dimon, J. (2023). Chairman & CEO Letter to Shareholders. JPMorgan Chase & Co.

Doerr, J. (2018). Measure what matters: How Google, Bono, and the Gates Foundation rock the world with OKRs. Penguin.

Gartenberg, C., Serafeim, G., & Sikochi, A. (2019). Corporate purpose and financial performance. Organization Science, 30(1), 1-18.

Gates, R. A. (2023). The Boeing 737 MAX crisis: A case study in engineering ethics and organizational failure. Journal of Business Ethics, 174(2), 341-358.

Goldman Sachs. (2023, October). Q3 2023 Earnings Report. Goldman Sachs Group, Inc.

Goleman, D. (2000). Leadership that gets results. Harvard Business Review, 78(2), 78-90.

Hambrick, D. C. & Frederickson, J. W. (2001). Are you sure you have a strategy? Academy of Management Perspectives, 15(4), 48-59.

Hastings, R. & Meyer, E. (2020). No rules rules: Netflix and the culture of reinvention. Penguin Press.

Heifetz, R. A., Grashow, A., & Linsky, M. (2009). The practice of adaptive leadership: Tools and tactics for changing your organization and the world. *Harvard Business Review Press*.

Huang, J. (2023, November 21). NVIDIA announces third quarter results. NVIDIA Newsroom.

Intel. (2023). 2022 Annual Report. Intel Corporation.

Jensen Huang, J. (2023). Transforming industries with AI: The NVIDIA way. *NVIDIA Annual Report*.

Joly, H. (2021). The heart of business: Leadership principles for the next era of capitalism. Harvard Business Review Press.

Joly, H. (2023). Purpose and profit: How business can lift up the world. Harvard Business Review Press.

Kanioura, A. (2023, March). PepsiCo's digital transformation: Building capability from within. CIO.com.

Kaplan, R. S. & Norton, D. P. (2008). The execution premium: Linking strategy to operations for competitive advantage. Harvard Business School Press.

Klein, D. A. (2019). Small giants: Companies that choose to be great instead of big. *Portfolio*.

Kotter, J. P. (2012). Leading change, with a new preface by the author. Harvard Business Review Press.

Lykke, A. F. (1989). Defining military strategy. Military Review, 69(5), 2-8.

REFERENCES

McGrath, R. G. (2013). The end of competitive advantage: How to keep your strategy moving as fast as your business. Harvard Business Review Press.

McGrath, R. G. (2019). Seeing around corners: How to spot inflection points in business before they happen. Houghton Mifflin Harcourt.

Microsoft. (2023, January 23). Microsoft and OpenAI extend partnership. Microsoft News.

Nadella, S. (2023, November 15). Satya Nadella at Microsoft Ignite: AI transforms everything. Microsoft Blog.

Nadella, S., Shaw, G., & Nichols, J. T. (2017). Hit refresh: The quest to rediscover Microsoft's soul and imagine a better future for everyone. Harper Business.

Nokia. (2021). The rise and fall of Nokia mobile phones. Nokia Corporation Historical Archive.

NVIDIA. (2023). 2023 Annual Report. NVIDIA Corporation.

Pick, T. (2023, October 13). Morgan Stanley Third Quarter 2023 Earnings Results. Morgan Stanley.

Reeves, M., Fæste, L., & Whitaker, K. (2020). Leading out of adversity. Harvard Business Review.

Reeves, M., Whitaker, K., & Fæste, L. (2021). Resilience in the face of disruption: Practical insights for organizations. Boston Consulting Group Insights Report.

Rudolph, J. W., & Repenning, N. P. (2002). Disaster dynamics: Understanding the role of organizational structure. *Academy of Management Review*, 27(1), 30-46.

Rumelt, R. P. (2011). Good strategy, bad strategy: The difference and why it matters. Crown Business.

Safian, R. (2017, January 16). Satya Nadella's got game. Fast Company.
Samsung Electronics. (2023, April 28). Samsung addresses ChatGPT security incident. Samsung Newsroom.

ServiceNow. (2023, December). Now Platform San Diego Release. ServiceNow Newsroom.

Sinek, S. (2009). Start with why: How great leaders inspire everyone to take action. Portfolio/Penguin.

Solomon, D. (2023, October 17). Goldman Sachs Reports Third Quarter 2023 Earnings. Goldman Sachs.

Su, L. (2023, October). AMD CEO Lisa Su on AI Strategy. AMD Blog.

Su, L. (2023). AMD's transformation: A case study in strategic leadership. Harvard Business Review, 101(6), 96-104.

Sull, D., Homkes, R., & Sull, C. (2015). Why strategy execution unravels - and what to do about it. Harvard Business Review, 93(3), 57-66.

Teece, D. J., Pisano, G., & Shuen, A. (1997). Dynamic capabilities and strategic management. Strategic Management Journal, 18(7), 509-533.

TSMC. (2023). Taiwan Semiconductor Manufacturing Company 2022 Annual Report. TSMC.

Walmart. (2023, September). Walmart accelerates AI transformation. Walmart Corporate.

REFERENCES

Walsh, B., Jamison, S., & Walsh, C. (2009). The score takes care of itself: My philosophy of leadership. Penguin.

Wells Fargo. (2023). 2022 Annual Report. Wells Fargo & Company.

Zolli, A. & Healy, A. M. (2012). Resilience: Why things bounce back. Simon & Schuster.

INDEX

Adaptive Leadership DNA, 19
Adaptive resilience, 7
Adobe, 27, 33, 38, 39, 43, 58, 66, 67, 119, 120, 121, 130, 131
AI Governance, 53
Airbnb, 5
Amazon, 6, 10, 11, 12, 21, 25, 30, 42, 44, 61, 65, 70, 73, 75, 82, 88, 97, 101, 119, 121, 124, 125, 138, 141
AMD, 25, 34, 69, 83, 86, 89, 91, 113, 123, 137, 141, 146
Anthropic, 60
Apple, 2, 6, 10, 13, 16, 49, 98, 99
Ballmer, Steve, 36, 73
Bastian, Ed, 20
Benioff, Marc, 59, 142
Best Buy, 3, 30, 42, 47, 49, 75
Bezos, Jeff, 22, 70
BlackBerry, 5, 42
Blockbuster, 2, 8, 11, 43, 96, 97, 106
Board level, 6, 21, 44, 57, 90, 110, 111
Boeing, 4, 69, 72, 87, 89, 93, 106, 109, 111, 112, 122, 142, 143
737 MAX, 4, 70, 93, 110, 142, 143
Borders Books, 6
Calendly, 131
Capability Building, 48, 55

Capability Mapping, 44
Capital One, 47
CD Projekt Red, 4
ChatGPT, 51, 57, 127, 146
Circuit City, 3
Cisco, 19
Citigroup, 59
Collaboration, 14, 33, 47, 48, 49, 51, 55, 62
Colonial Pipeline, 23
Continuous Learning Loops, 33
Cook, Tim, 98
Copper CRM, 130
COVID-19, 16, 20, 23, 31, 41, 99, 128, 142
C-suite, 1, 2, 9, 10, 12, 13, 15, 19, 21, 57, 70, 90, 111
Cultural Adaptation, 55
Cultural Coherence, 23, 25
Cultural Stagnation, 74
CVS Health, 41
Deep Redundancy, 22, 25
Delta Airlines, 20, 25, 43
Dimon, Jamie, 51, 113, 114
Ends, 7, 9, 10, 11, 12, 13, 15, 17
Ends, Ways, and Means, 7, 9, 12, 13, 15, 130
Figma, 130, 131
Ford Motor Company, 9
Gelsinger, Pat, 69, 81

General Electric, 5, 29, 46, 75, 76, 77, 85, 87, 112
General Motors, 45, 94, 138
Generative AI, vii, 51
Goldman Sachs, 51, 64, 143, 146
Google, 54, 56, 60, 74, 143
Gorman, James, 56
Hastings, Reed, 11
Huang, Jensen, 54, 91
IBM, 54, 60, 63, 65, 87, 104, 123, 127
  Watson, 54
Immelt, Jeff, 29, 46, 77, 85, 112
Implementation, 15, 28
Intel, 25, 34, 37, 66, 67, 69, 70, 81, 83, 86, 123, 137, 144
J.C. Penney, 13
Jasper AI, 127
Jobs, Steve, 6
Johnson, Ron, 13
Joly, Hubert, 30, 42, 47, 75, 144
JP Morgan Chase, 46, 51, 79, 84, 113, 114
Kanioura, Athina, 116
Kodak, 5, 15, 39, 49, 109, 123
Kraft Heinz, 104, 105
Krishna, Arvind, 54
Krzanich, Brian, 69
Lafley, A.G., 21
Leadership Alignment, 34
Lehman Brothers, 1
Linear, 132
Linear Thinking, 32, 63, 64, 94, 96, 97, 100, 102, 105, 106, 137, 138, 139

Loom, 129
Means, 9, 10, 11, 12, 13, 14, 15, 16, 17
Meta, 53
Metrics, 1, 2, 5, 6, 7, 8, 9, 10, 15, 17, 28, 30, 31, 32, 39, 45, 47
Metrics Mirage, The, 30
Microsoft, 2, 4, 7, 10, 12, 14, 15, 16, 23, 24, 25, 28, 30, 32, 35, 36, 43, 44, 45, 48, 49, 52, 53, 54, 55, 57, 59, 60, 61, 62, 65, 66, 69, 73, 74, 80, 82, 84, 85, 87, 88, 89, 91, 102, 103, 104, 106, 111, 114, 115, 117, 118, 119, 121, 122, 125, 130, 134, 137, 138, 142, 145
Military planners, 12
Morgan Stanley, 56, 57, 65, 145
Muilenburg, Dennis, 72, 73
Mulally, Alan, 9, 28, 29
Mulcahy, Anne, 10, 26, 27, 35
Nadella, Satya, 4, 7, 10, 12, 14, 23, 24, 25, 30, 36, 43, 44, 45, 59, 69, 73, 74, 82, 84, 87, 89, 91, 102, 111, 114, 115, 117, 122, 125, 137, 145, 146
NASA, 28
Netflix, 2, 8, 11, 24, 96, 97, 139, 141, 143
Network-Centric Operations, 20, 25
Nike, 99, 100, 106
Nokia, 2, 42, 71
Nooyi, Indra, 104
Notion, 128, 130

INDEX

NVIDIA, 54, 63, 66, 67, 87, 89, 91, 118, 124, 144, 145
Old Tech Governance, 53
OpenAI, 51, 52, 55, 58, 59, 60, 63, 141, 145
Oracle, 62, 65, 66, 128
PepsiCo, 104, 105, 106, 116
Pick, Ted, 65
Process Integration, 55
Procter & Gamble, 21, 25, 38
Connect + Develop, 38
Program Trap, The, 29
Radio Shack, 47
Regular Reality Checks, 33
Retool, 133
Rite Aid, 41
Salesforce, 37, 59, 60, 65, 66, 67, 130, 142
Samsung, 57, 71
SAP, 65
Sears, 6, 94, 95, 96, 106, 138
ServiceNow, 120
Snowflake, 62
Solomon, David, 51, 64, 146
Square, 59
Stable Diffusion, 58
Starbucks, 32, 141
Status quo, 2
Stripe, 59
Su, Lisa, 34, 83, 86, 89, 91, 113, 114, 123, 146
Sunk Cost Fallacy, 3
Sustainability Deception, 3, 137
SWOT, 44
Taiwan Semiconductor Manufacturing Company, 22, 25, 34, 71, 123, 137, 146
Target, 56
Tesla, 139
Toast, 128
Toyota, 21, 49, 94, 138
Toys "R" Us, 11, 42
Traditional resilience, 2, 4, 5, 7, 8
Under Armour, 99, 100
United Airlines, 4
Vercel, 129, 132
VUCA, 4
Walmart, 56, 95, 96, 146
Ways, 7, 9, 10, 11, 12, 13, 14, 15, 16, 17
Wells Fargo, 47, 59, 147
Xerox, 6, 10, 26, 27, 35
Yahoo, 49
Zapier, 134
Zoom, 19

www.ingramcontent.com/pod-product-compliance
Lightning Source LLC
Chambersburg PA
CBHW052317220526
45472CB00001B/158